Beyond Christian Zionism

Beyond Christian Zionism

—— *A Travelogue of a Former Ideologue* ——

Ian Stackhouse

CASCADE *Books* • Eugene, Oregon

BEYOND CHRISTIAN ZIONISM
A Travelogue of a Former Ideologue

Cascade Books
An Imprint of Wipf and Stock Publishers
199 W. 8th Ave., Suite 3
Eugene, OR 97401

www.wipfandstock.com

PAPERBACK ISBN: 979-8-3852-0359-8
HARDCOVER ISBN: 979-8-3852-0360-4
EBOOK ISBN: 979-8-3852-0361-1

Cataloguing-in-Publication data:

Names: Stackhouse, Ian [author].

Title: Beyond Christian Zionism : a travelogue of a former ideologue / by Ian Stackhouse.

Description: Eugene, OR: Cascade Books, 2024 | Includes bibliographical references.

Identifiers: ISBN 979-8-3852-0359-8 (paperback) | ISBN 979-8-3852-0360-4 (hardcover) | ISBN 979-8-3852-0361-1 (ebook)

Subjects: LCSH: Christian Zionism. | Arab-Israeli conflict. | Judaism (Christian theology). | Zionism. | Jews—Restoration.

Classification: DS150.5 S73 2024 (paperback) | DS150.5 (ebook)

VERSION NUMBER 05/13/24

To my beloved Chichester Cathedral

This one was born there.
And of Zion, it shall be said, every man is born in it.

Psalm 87:4–5

Contents

Preface

It is strange how anniversaries seem to trigger my writing projects. *Letters to a Young Pastor: Reflections on Leadership, Community, and the Gospel of Grace* (Eugene: Cascade, 2019) drew its inspiration from a desire to mark twenty-five years of Christian ministry. Likewise, *Praying Psalms: A Personal Journey through the Psalter* (Eugene: Cascade, 2018) arose from a decade of routinely praying all one hundred and fifty Psalms, once a month. These landmarks clearly lodge in my soul as a kind of creative spark. No surprise, therefore, that my trip to Israel in the January of 2023, forty years almost to the month when I touched down at Ben Gurion airport as a young nineteen-year-old, should be a catalyst for *Beyond Christian Zionism: A Travelogue of a Former Ideologue*. Forty years has, of course, a biblical feel about it, and my adoption of it as a timeframe for my reflections may well come across as conceited. But what those forty years represent, with regard to the matter of Christian Zionism, is a very personal journey away from ideological fundamentalism towards what I believe to be a far more considered, biblically coherent position about the land, the gospel, and the people of God.

Given the reflective nature of the writing—as close as I might get to a memoir—I offer it as the third in a trilogy of books with

Cascade. If *Letters to a Young Pastor* is a reflection on my experience as a pastor, and *Praying Psalms* a reflection on my prayer life, then *Beyond Christian Zionism* is a reflection on what it means to be an exegete, an ecumenist, and activist. Christian Zionism is not the only theological/political issue in which I give expression to those things. Over the years, I have been trying to exercise the same diligence on a whole range of matters. But it would be true to say that this is an issue that I have wrestled with for the longest, and one that requires perhaps the greatest sensitivity.

Which brings me to a rather more sinister anniversary, and one which I am bound to refer to before signing off: namely, the surprise attack on Israel by Hamas on Saturday, October 7, 2023, fifty years plus a day since the Yom Kippur War, and what many already refer to as Israel's 9/11. As it was, I had already submitted a first completed draft of the book to the publishers at the end of September, satisfied with what I had written and hopeful that it would resonate with the ever-changing landscape of the Arab-Israeli conflict. By every measurement, however, this was different. Indeed, I would go so far as to say that the barbarism of Hamas, and its avowed genocidal intent, is not germane to the politics of the region, nor to the Palestinian people as a whole, but something introduced from outside, namely Iran.

That the events of that terrible day focus on the Israeli town of Ashkelon and its vicinity is poignant, as it is where my journey began forty years ago, and where I left a bit of my heart. As the story unfolded, I found myself becoming more and more distressed. It is the biggest single incident of Jewish killings since the Second World War. But then, as it became clear that the Israeli response to Gaza was going to result in the deaths of thousands of innocent Palestinians, I found myself becoming more and more dismayed. Who knows where it will all end? By the time my little book makes publication, things will no doubt have changed again. Hence, I decided not to rewrite the book, but leave the manuscript as it was, trusting that the moments of prescience in the narrative—and there are a few—would indicate my awareness of how volatile things are. No one could have foreseen the scale and brutality of what happened on that Saturday morning—of course not—nor the massive failure of security it represents. In many ways it takes us into a whole new landscape. But what is so depressing is that the new landscape will undoubtedly resonate with the existential fears of both communities—the Holocaust and the *Nakba*—and therefore perpetuate, understandably so, the political mythologies of both sides.

As will become clear from the introduction, one of my problems with Christian Zionism, which after all is the focus of the book, is that it contributes to the conflict by adding a mythology all of its own, and thereby legitimizing, in a perverse kind of way, a retaliatory violence that in any other context we would regard as excessive. Israel has a right to defend herself. The Christian community should stand in solidarity with the Jewish people. On Sunday, October 8, with news still emerging of the most barbarous jihadism, I led the congregation at Millmead in prayers for Israel, and for the Jewish community here in the UK. It is imperative that we do. We also prayed, however, for restraint, because if we know anything from the message of Jesus, as opposed to the message of extremist Zionism, we know that violence begets violence. Indeed, if there is a response that the Christian community should make at this time it is that of peacebuilding. In my opinion, one of the reasons that the region is so vulnerable to extremism, on both sides, is because the peace process, so called, has almost entirely broken down. And if we are to retrieve anything from the wreckage of this tragedy, and if the church is to make any contribution, may it be this: not the polemic of binary thinking, but the often misunderstood yet courageous task of building bridges. As Jesus said, in the context of oppression and violence, "Blessed are the peacemakers, for they will be called sons of God."[1]

---

1. Matt 5:9.

Acknowledgments

MY THANKS TO THE Rev. Dr. Daniel Inman, Canon Chancellor of Chichester Cathedral, for creating a most delightful post of theologian-in-residence for the summer of my sabbatical in 2023. It was not a hardship to preach for my keep. Indeed, there were times when I was sitting in the library that I truly thought I was in heaven. The sound of the choir rehearsing Frank Martin's Mass for Double Choir for the Summer Choirs Festival (Chichester, Winchester, and Salisbury) will stay with me for a long time. I don't know how much longer we shall have our little house in Chichester, but it has been so special to be a part of the Cathedral community for this brief period. I shall miss being at the 8 a.m. Eucharist in the Lady chapel, and then coffee afterwards at Greggs.

As to those who have influenced the writing of this book, my immense thanks to Professor Melissa Raphael, a long-standing friend from our university days, a companion in the faith in so many ways, and such a helpful critic. As always, her erudition far surpasses mine. In conversation with her, I am acutely conscious how fumbling my sentences are. But I am glad for the time spent together in dialogue, and always richer for the sharing of ideas. Without her wisdom, the book would likely have ended up more of a polemic than a memoir. That she was willing to offer her comments, even though there will be much here in the final manuscript that still irks her, is testament to her graciousness.

My thanks also to my good friend Rev. Dr. Alasdair Black, Senior Minster at Stirling Baptist Church, for taking me and two of my sons to Israel in 2014. Our whistle stop tour, which included time in East Jerusalem, Bethlehem, and Nablus, was so important in the forming of my own response to the realities of occupation. It was especially poignant since I was able to reunite on this trip with my old friend Shai, as well as his dear mother, Ruti. I dare not think what he will make of my reflections here. He has lived through these decades whereas I am simply a bystander. But I hope he will register, despite my critique, my deep affection for his country. I hope the same for the congregation I serve at Millmead. Had they known what I was writing on my three-month sabbatical, maybe they would have withdrawn the offer. On the other hand, maybe they will be relieved that I have finally come clear on what I think about this issue which has been so much part of the spirituality of the church. I hope no one else leaves Millmead over it. Too many people, sadly, have forsaken deep bonds of Christian fellowship for the sake of this ideology. But if they do, I hope they will at least be clearer as to why people like me are so reluctant to take up their cause.

I should also like to include in these acknowledgments Simon Walsh, my long-standing friend and partner in ministry, and his friends Gregor and Ivy. Their desire to facilitate my stay in Jerusalem in January 2023, including a special pass into the Knesset, was so generous, and proved to be just the spark I needed to begin writing. It wasn't long after my return that the words began to flow.

My final thanks are to my researcher, Nathaniel, who has supplied me with many up-to-date articles and has been a very helpful sounding board for some of my ideas. His own time in Israel, courtesy of a scholarship with the Jerusalem Trust, gave him first-hand experience of this remarkable country. The views expressed in this book are mine, but my thanks go to Nathaniel, and indeed to many others, for the encouragement to write on such a controversial subject. The protests this summer against the Netanyahu government's plans to curtail the powers of the Supreme Court are unprecedented in the history of this young democracy and remind us that there is nothing more topical than what happens on the streets of Jerusalem.

The Feast of the Transfiguration 2023

Introduction

IT JUST SO HAPPENS that my first visit to Israel was on my nineteenth birthday, February 26, 1983. Courtesy of a scholarship with The Friends of Israel Educational Foundation, a pressure group founded by the ever youthful John Levy, ten of us arrived late at night in Jerusalem on the Feast of Purim, checked into a hostel near the Jaffa Gate, and woke the next morning to the unexpected sight of snow.[1] Given that it was winter, and that Jerusalem is high up in the hills, snow is hardly surprising. But it certainly lingers in my memory of what was to be the beginning of lifelong relationship with Israel. It is a relationship that has swung over the last forty years from an initial love affair, all the way to outright despair, which is often what transpires when you idealize something, and then back to what I think is a more mature relationship: one that is able to hold in tension the complexity of the politics and theology of this unique land, and celebrate Israel, strangely enough, as something like home. It is how I have arrived at that place that drives the narrative of the book: how a young idealistic new convert to evangelical Christian faith in the early

---

1. The Bridge for Britain scheme, promoted by The Friends of Israel Educational Trust, ran for several years, giving six-month scholarships to gap year students wanting to experience life in Israel.

eighties swallowed whole the Christian Zionist narrative, eventually spat much of it out, and then, having recovered from this extreme reaction, tried to foster an understanding of the land of Israel that is honouring of its remarkable history, sympathetic of the Palestinian dimension of that history, and then, most importantly, re-imagined in the light of the incarnation.

In setting out such an agenda, I am anxious to make it clear from the very beginning—and will no doubt reiterate this many times—that I do not repudiate Israel's right to exist. God forbid. Nor do I believe that Israel is now replaced by the church. I find both of those thoughts as odious as any Christian Zionist would find them. According to those celebrated chapters of Romans 9–11, the Jews have yet a remarkable role to play in the unfolding of God's drama. Indeed, Jews are a remarkable people, full stop. Their contribution to the world is incalculable. And if Christian Zionism is about acknowledging that, then I am a devotee. Where I depart from Christian Zionism, however, and one of the reasons why I feel compelled to go into print about it after all this time, concerns the theological weight one attaches to the Jewish return to the land of Israel. For Christian Zionists, the return is integral, if not the actual reference, to the regrafting of the natural olive branches into their own olive tree, to use St. Paul's image.[2] In most strands of Christian Zionism, the return is prerequisite for the return of Christ. For evangelical Christians like me, however, the restoration to the land for the sake of Jewish conversion and end-time apocalyptic is problematic, since it not only contributes to the political stalemate between Israelis and Palestinians, but also counters the undoubted centrifugal thrust of the gospel out to the nations.

As much as I have tried over the years to reconcile these ideas and marry together Jewish territorialism with the Christian gospel, I have come to the conclusion, as will quickly become apparent, that they are incompatible for the simple reason, as William Davies argues, that the incarnation of Jesus effectively

2. Rom 11:17–24.

desacralizes the notion of territory.[3] Indeed, the presence of Jesus desacralizes not just Jewish territorialism, but Samaritan and pagan as well. The opening chapters of John's Gospel make clear that something very expansive is happening in the ministry of the Word made flesh that will take the locus of God's covenant promises away from land and towards a person. To reinvigorate the land, therefore, with eschatological and sometimes millenarian significance, as Christian Zionists do, is not only retrograde but also, in a strange kind of irony, unevangelistic, since it tends to downplay conversion for the sake of apocalyptic fulfillment.[4] In short, the prophecies concerning the land end up as more important than the salvation of souls—both Jew and gentile.

I am sure this is not always the case. After all, Christian Zionism is a peculiarly Protestant evangelical phenomenon. I have no doubt Christian Zionists are passionate about Jesus. But if the popular literature is anything to go by, classical evangelical doctrines are so often eclipsed by the theological interest that gathers around the vision to see the restoration of Israel. Furthermore, in the ongoing conflict with the indigenous Arab population, there is little doubt that the territorial vision of Christian Zionism has hindered rather than helped any long-term political solution. The nomenclature of Judea and Samaria as an alternative to what is more commonly referred to as the West Bank may sound innocuous to some but, as with all political re-naming, the endorsement of a Greater Israel by Christian Zionists negates any idea of a two-state solution. It represents the ascendency of Jewish ethnicity over pluralistic democracy, and is a challenge, as I will attempt to show, to what John Yoder calls "the politics of Jesus." If the Jesus revolution was from the very beginning about the creation of

---

3. Davies, *Gospel and the Land.*

4. As Stanley and Munro Price have shown, the tension between straightforward Evangelicals who did not believe in the imminence of the Second Coming and simply wished to preach Christianity to the Jews, versus millenarians who believed it was imminent and supported conversion and restoration in order to hasten it, was present in the London Society for Promoting Christianity among the Jews, which formed in 1809. See Price, *Road to the Apocalypse,* 17–19.

heterogenous communities—the destruction of dividing walls of hostility between Jews and gentiles[5]—the movement of Christian Zionism has been in the other direction: a reinforcement of divisions, including the building of actual walls.

Having crossed those physical barriers several times and having spent a significant amount of time in the land, I am not about to make a simple comparison with the state of apartheid that existed in South Africa for much of the twentieth century. The history of the Arab-Israeli conflict is too complex, and too context specific, to allow for such an easy swipe.[6] What I will observe, however, is a growing sense of betrayal among Palestinian Christians who see Christian Zionism as an oppressive theology that helps solidify present divides rather than challenge them.[7] It is complex, to be sure. In entering the fray, I fear that no amount of nuance will do justice to all the issues. What I do want to state from the very beginning, however, is that there is something radically new about the Christian gospel that should call to account all political, theological and social constructs, particularly those, like Christian Zionism, that have proven so influential. It is that radical newness that I want to explore in this book.

A word about Jesus the Jew. Contrary to what one might expect in a critique of Christian Zionism, I do not intend at any point in this discussion to erase the Jewishness of Jesus. In the current melee of identity politics, Jewish broadcaster David Baddiel is right to insist on this classification.[8] Indeed, I intend to

---

5. Eph 2:14–16.

6. There are several titles in the literature where the word apartheid features, including Jimmy Carter's memoir of the Arab-Israel confrontation, *Palestine Peace not Apartheid*. See also White, *Israeli Apartheid*. Even though White insists on using the term apartheid to describe Israel's treatment of Palestinians, he does admit that there are significant differences to the institutionalized race discrimination that was legalized by the white minority in South Africa.

7. Braverman, *Wall in Jerusalem*, 104–49. With reference to the political catastrophe that describes the plight of the Palestinians in 1948—the *Nakba*—Braverman describes Christian Zionism as a theological catastrophe.

8. Baddiel, *Jews Don't Count*, 80–83.

strengthen that identity in the last section of the book. For me, the universality of the gospel and the particularity of the Jewish Jesus are not mutually exclusive. The genius of the gospel is that it holds both together. But Jewishness, as Baddiel himself argues with respect to his own concerns about growing antisemitism in Europe, does not necessarily have to equate with a particular ideology—that is, nationalist Zionist ideology—concerning the land. To insist that the two are inseparable is to coerce Jesus into a strangely militant figure, and a trope that clashes with his message of peace as found in the historic gospels. In my estimation, as will become clear in the following chapters, Christian Zionism, both in its British version as well as its American version, skirts close to being "another gospel."

To state the theological issues in these bold terms, and to insist thereby on the utter uniqueness of Christ, is not a case of replacement, as Christian Zionists are so quick to accuse. At no point in this book do I posit the church as the replacement of Israel. Rather, I am wanting to celebrate the climax of the covenant story of God in the person of Jesus Christ, whose universal supremacy relativizes, if not makes obsolete, all former arrangements.[9] The gospels bear witness to this. The New Testament unpacks the implications for that on a full range of matters, from ethics all the way to ecclesiology. Hence, what I am seeking to offer, by way of reflection on those same scriptures, is a critique of what I have come to regard as a sub-Christian ideology, and an articulation, in its place, of what many believe to be a more equitable, generous, gospel centred approach.

I am of course aware of the dangers. In trying to write my way through the impasse of ideologies and on towards something that I would regard as distinctively Christian, I run the risk of being attacked from both sides. My subject matter does not allow for a non-partisan approach. But then again, in venturing into this field, I may as well admit now that I am not claiming neutrality, any more than I am trying to achieve balance. In contexts like this one (and I can think of a good few others), balance is not an option. As I

9. See Wright, *Climax of the Covenant.*

have discovered many times as a pastoral leader in the church, certain issues are so important that some measure of commitment is required. We may of course want to reassess those commitments in the light of further reflection. I have done that many times. To not be willing to reassess is arrogant. But to not commit in the first place, and to pretend that every conflict of ideas can be ameliorated by the notion of moral equivalence—the idea that both arguments have equal credibility—seems to me a coward's way out and, furthermore, runs the risk of confusing everyone.

John le Carré's novel *The Little Drummer Girl* is a case in point.[10] I reread it in preparation for writing this book. Centred on the conflicting emotions of Charlie, a young English actress with left-wing sympathies whom Mossad have wooed to lead them to Khalil, a Palestinian terrorist, the book is more a suspense thriller than a political statement. Indeed, le Carré is insistent that the novel is morally and politically neutral. But herein lies the problem. In a conflict where both sides claim to be the victims of injustice, the stance of moral equivalence—that is, the attempt to be balanced in one's judgment of the situation—runs the risk of upsetting everyone. In the case of *The Little Drummer Girl*, Israelis accuse le Carré of humanizing Palestinian terrorists in the novel; just as Palestinians get incensed every time the Jewish plight is accorded equal dignity.

What is interesting about this matter, and pertinent I believe to my own methodology here, is that the publication of *The Little Drummer Girl* took place at around the same time as one of the worst atrocities in the history of the Israeli Defence Force (IDF), namely the massacre of Palestinian refugees in the Sabra and Shatila camp in Beirut. I recall the outrage in the international community because I arrived in Israel in the February of 1983, just five months after the event. John le Carré admitted himself that had he still been in the writing stage the novel would have been a lot angrier about the injustices perpetrated against the Palestinians, although my own reading of *The Little Drummer Girl* left me in no doubt already as to where le Carré's sympathies lay, and possibly

10. le Carré, *Little Drummer Girl*.

why he wrote the book in the first place. It is well known, for example, that the title of the book is a reference to the American journalist Janet Lee Stevens, who died in the 1983 bombing of the US Embassy in Beirut. Stevens had given le Carré a tour of Sabra and Shatila in 1982, having become something of an advocate for the residents there, most of whom were refugees from 1948.[11]

To get to my point, even if le Carré is politically neutral, as he claims to be, the novel provides, at the very least, a challenging exposure, through the conflicted loyalties of the central character, of the substantive issues that the modern democracy of Israel faces as it tries to make its way in the global culture. My own goal is to do something similar for the evangelical Christian community: to raise questions about the embedded theology of the Christian Zionist movement; to challenge its apocalypticism as singularly unhelpful in the seemingly hopeless quest for a political solution; and to offer, as someone who has journeyed for over four decades with this particular issue, a way forward that is judicious, merciful and, most importantly, reflective of the central themes of Jesus' ministry.

Given the way I write theology, which tends towards a dialectical approach, I am unlikely to avoid to the charge of supersessionism; and I suspect, sadly, that I may well have to deal with the charge of antisemitism. But as Rosie Jones argued, amidst the storm around her television documentary about disability, at least I have written it in the way that is true to my experience of this matter. Christian Zionism has been ever present in the churches I have had the privilege to lead. Until now, it is not something I have wanted to write about. But for whatever reason, and however foolish this project is, this seems to be the right time to put on record what I think about the matter. Much as I love Israel, and much as I respect Christians, as well as Jews of course, who hold

11. Such was her support for the Palestinian cause, Stevens was once charged with being a "partisan journalist". It would be too simple to see Charlie as a cipher for Stevens. Her character is most definitely a fiction. Even so, Charlie's awakening in the novel to the Palestinian cause certainly resonates with aspects of Stevens' political sympathies. 'The Little Drummer Girl' is, after all, the affectionate name given to Stevens by the Palestinians.

a central place for the land in their eschatology, what should not be glossed over any longer, much less endorsed, is the aggressive militarism, if not exceptionalism, that underpins the on-going occupation of the West Bank and Gaza. To not speak to this decidedly un-Jewish response to the stranger, for fear of criticism, or for fear of vilification, is not something I am willing to do any longer. And to not at least try to articulate an alternative theology of the land that is congruent with the spectacularly new thing that occurs in the gospel of Jesus Christ strikes me as cowardly. At time of writing, the issues in Israel could not be more vivid. The prospect of a political breakthrough is unlikely. If anything, something like another intifada appears unavoidable. But the intractability of the situation should not prevent, in my opinion, serious reflection from within the Christian community.

That my own work takes on the nature of a travelogue is because I felt this was the best way to express my heart on the matter. I have collected enough books over the years to be able to write something more academic. But rather than write a purely theological book, of which there are many, or attempt to offer a political solution, which would be inadvisable, I felt I could make a better contribution by writing something part memoir, part spirituality, part history, part theology—as I say, something like a travelogue—thus leaving much of the commentary about the literature, which is extensive, to the footnotes.

In no way do I claim the final word. As with all my books, I hope it will stir up debate. I hope it will give permission. And maybe, in a very Jewish way, the book might open up an "argument for the sake of heaven." It is written by someone who holds dear Dietrich Bonhoeffer's maxim that "only he who shouts for the Jews is permitted to sing the Gregorian chants." Given the growing spectre of antisemitism in Europe, I have a feeling that may be put to the test. On the other hand, I do not believe that criticism of Israel is *ipso facto* a form of antisemitism. I can see how it might be. There are those who are adept at hiding their antisemitism in all kinds of ways. But to state unequivocally that *any* criticism of the state of Israel is, by definition, a form of racism against Jewish people, is not only a simplification of the relationship between Israel and the diaspora, but also a subtle form of cancelling. As with so many debates now, what we need is not a cancel culture, but a few faithful friends who are willing to speak. And if I am accused of antisemitism, I shall take refuge in my beloved Marc Chagall, whose window here at Chichester Cathedral is one of its many Jewish connections.[12]

Like many Jews of his generation, notes Jackie Wullschlager, Chagall found it hard to admit that he didn't feel entirely comfortable in Israel.[13] Although his visit to the land in 1931 ignited his passion to paint the biblical narrative—a project he completed in 1952—it was the shtetl of his childhood that was his inspiration. Indeed, he found it hard to identify with Sabra mindset, even if he could admire it. For Chagall, Israel was future oriented, in contrast to his art which was located in memory.[14] This did not stop him supporting Israel. I have seen with my own eyes the twelve windows at the Hadassah hospital in Ein Kerem that Chagall bequeathed to the nation, as well as the enormous tapestries at the Knesset depicting the aliyah of both Ashkenazi Jews and Sephardi Jews to the land of promise. There is no question that Chagall believed in Israel's reason to exist. In one of the windows that was smashed during the Six-Day War, Chagall worked into his repair, at his own expense, a shard of glass from the bombing. But in a strange kind of way his biography, which spanned the Russian revolution, Fascism in Europe, and then exile in the United States, made him singularly unable to embrace a Zionist vision, preferring instead to place his unmistakably Jewish art in service to a common humanity. For Chagall, the Bible is a universal story not despite its particularity but precisely because of its particularity.

12. The others being the paintings of the Jewish refugee, Hans Feibusch, and the music of Leonard Bernstein. I was delighted to discover, only recently, that Robert Potter, the architect of the Millmead Centre which opened in 1972, was pivotal to the commissioning of the Chagall window at Chichester Cathedral. For a fuller account, see Hussey, *Patron of Art*, 138–46.

13. Wullschlager, *Chagall*, 461.

14. Alexander, *Marc Chagall*, 417.

I would like to think I am trying to achieve something similar here: a travelogue that both celebrates the unique and particular story of God's relationship to Israel but also, on account of the life, death and resurrection of Jesus of Nazareth, takes that story and sends it out the world. If that is regarded by some as antisemitic because it fails to fully endorse a Zionist vision, then so be it. There is only so much one can do to defend oneself. For my part, I would like to see *Beyond Christian Zionism* as a full flowering of the Hebrew scriptures, bringing to completion a message of salvation that is truly for all people of the world. As Hebraist Robert Alter notes in his commentary on the Psalm 87:4–5, which I have placed as the epigraph of my book: "The wording is certainly cryptic, but it might convey a universalist message about Jerusalem."[15] As the psalm intimates, and as Jesus makes explicit, Zion was never meant to be a nationalistic enclave, but the source of living water for all peoples of the world.

15. Alter, *Book of Psalms*, 307.

Part One

Encountering Christian Zionism

A Strange and Personal Journey

IN THE SUMMER OF 2003, having just returned with my family from three months in Cincinnati, I was invited to meet with the elders of Guildford Baptist Church, known more popularly in the town as Millmead. They were in search of a new pastoral leader, having been without for a few years. Following a protracted period of discernment, I was voted in at a church congregational meeting (which is how Baptists do these things), taking up my post on Palm Sunday 2004.

In terms of the subject of our book, the significance, as well as the irony, of the appointment is that for a period in the seventies, under the leadership of David Pawson, Millmead was the epicenter of Christian Zionism in the UK.[1] In fact, it was the epi-

1. See Pawson, *Defending Christian Zionism.* David Pawson claims that he was provoked to write the book in response to the work of Stephen Sizer, an evangelical Anglican who rejects Christian Zionism and who in January 2023 was officially prohibited from licensed ministry in the Church of England until 2030 on account of what was deemed antisemitic activity. For an introduction to his views on Christian Zionism, see Sizer, *Christian Zionism.*

center not just of Christian Zionism but of Charismatic Renewal; but since Charismatic Renewal at that time included a very strong pro-Israel strand, David's Christian Zionism was not out of place.[2] The few times that any of the new churches, so-called, promoted a pro-Palestinian stance, they were summarily criticized.[3]

As was the case with many single issues in Christian theology, including the matter of women in leadership, David had strong views. Regarding Israel, he propagated a strongly held conviction among Christian Zionists that the creation of the state of Israel in 1948 was a fulfillment of Old Testament prophecy. So strongly did he hold this view that by the time he left Millmead in the late seventies some people felt that the Israel theme was almost more important than the gospel. It wasn't of course. David was more than able to differentiate the two and keep the gospel central. Furthermore, he had some reservations himself about certain aspects of Christian Zionism. We discussed this once at his home near Basingstoke. But the fact that there was even a perception of this, not to mention the fact that even by the time I arrived in 2003 the church was still festooned with various Jewish artifacts—a menorah, some memorial plates inscribed in Hebrew, to name a few—indicates how central Israel was at that time to the spiritual vision of the church, and how problematic that would prove to future generations who might want to challenge the Christian Zionist hermeneutic. Alas, I can think of at least a dozen families who moved on from Millmead once they discovered that I was not going to promote Christian Zionism in my teaching. Only recently, a Baptist minister told me of a congregant who came to see him about leaving the church. When he pressed the person as to what it was that was causing them to feel so unsettled, it was the lack of prayer for Israel that was the presenting reason. It still lingers.

2. See Hocken, *Glory and the Shame*, 133–47, for an example of the confluence of renewal and Jewish messianism.

3. I recall a conversation in the mid-eighties with Bryn Jones, one of the apostles of the Restoration movement, in which he recounted the numerous hate letters that their magazine *Restoration* (Harvestime Publications) received following a series of pro-Palestinian articles.

Why anyone would leave a church community over an ideology that, for the most part, barely touches our everyday lives is hard to understand. Such is the importance of Israel, however, in the end-time eschatology of Christian Zionists, and the consequent judgment on anyone who fails to keep faith with Israel, then I guess there is a certain logic to it. In other words, if you believe that God blesses those who bless Israel, and curses those who curse Israel, which is standard fare in Christian Zionism,[4] then where do you go if you hear someone criticize the Israeli government, for example, or the military?[5] The room for manoeuvre is very small. If your pastor is less than passionate about Israel, or even some ways critical of Israel's security measures, what choice do you have but to denounce them?[6] Or if not denounce them, then leave. Fortunately, or unfortunately, depending on which way you look at it, there are always plenty of churches one can transfer to. Last count, Guildford had over forty churches. One or two of those are particularly focused on supporting Israel. So that is where most of our disaffected Christian Zionists have gone.

The irony in all of this is that twenty years earlier, just after that first impressionable visit to Israel in 1983, I was completely convinced by the narrative of Christian Zionism. As a result of a six month scholarship, first teaching in a High School in the coastal city of Ashkelon, and then farming at Kibbutz Alumot in Galilee,[7] I was so immersed in the teaching and literature that ac-

4. The critical biblical text for Christian Zionists is Gen 12:3.

5. For a classic statement of this blessing/curse formula, see Prince, *Why Israel?*, 79–82. It ought to be noted that Derek Prince extended this formula to everyday matters beyond the issues around the state of Israel, often with devastating pastoral consequences.

6. For an example of this invective, see the pamphlet by Ken Burnett, *Nation Called by God*. The author states: "Within the church as a whole, the life-giving breath of prayer that we in Britain have been called to release over Israel has been stifled and silenced through the distorted teaching imposed upon God's people. For this (Replacement Theology), God will hold His shepherds responsible."

7. It was only through watching the Netflix biographical *Never Stop Dreaming: The Life and Legacy of Shimon Peres* (2022) that I discovered that the former prime minister of Israel helped found Kibbutz Alumot, which is just off

companied this particular theology that had I gone to Millmead at that point in my journey—even as a congregant, let alone as a pastor—I too would have promoted it as a central plank of the church's mission. The early eighties were the apogee of Christian Zionism. This was the era of Bible teachers like Lance Lambert and Derek Prince;[8] this was a time when messianic congregations were springing up all over Israel; the International Christian Embassy opened in Jerusalem in 1980, "recognising the modern-day restoration of Israel as the faithfulness of God to keep His ancient covenant promises to the Jewish people." Indeed, by the time I arrived in Jerusalem in 1983, the Feast of Tabernacles was already developing as a focal point for Christians around the world who wanted to stand in solidarity with Israel. What chance did I have? The Christian Zionist narrative was very persuasive, not to mention very welcome to a right-wing Likud government that was looking for allies to support its expansionist Greater Israel program. The fact that in 1982 Prime Minister Menachem Begin presented evangelist Jerry Falwell, leader of the Moral Majority, with a medal of the Jabotinsky Order tells you a great deal about the growing connection between Christian fundamentalism in North America and right-wing Zionism.

As I recall it, the beliefs of Christian Zionists at that time, both here and in the States, centered on a series of sequiturs: that the return of Jews to the land of Israel was indeed a fulfillment of biblical prophecy; that the covenant made with Abraham concerning the land is inviolable; and that Israel, therefore, was justified in building settlements on the West Bank. More pronounced versions of this ideology also promoted the rebuilding of the temple in Jerusalem, along with the reintroduction of certain religious laws. So watertight was this argument that it was hard to gainsay it

---

the southern tip of the Sea of Galilee. Having closed for a period of time, it was reopened in 1969 by a group of Argentinian Jews. By the time I arrived there, it would be fair to say that some of the ideals of the kibbutz movement had eroded. More positively, much of my work during my time there involved installing a drip system, pioneered in Israel, for irrigating the cotton fields. It was impressive, to say the least.

8. See Lambert, *Battle for Israel*; Prince, *Last Word on the Middle East*.

without feeling that one was betraying a very sacred cause. I know this both as an insider and as an eventual dissenter. To detract from the narrative even to a slight degree was dangerous. And to suggest that maybe fascination with all things Israel was going just a bit too far and starting to eclipse the gospel of Jesus—which is how I started to see it in the late eighties—was to be guilty of the ultimate sin which is replacement theology.

Replacement theology is a belief—used by Christian Zionists as a derogatory term—that the promise God made with Israel concerning the land has been replaced by a very different, more spiritual kind of covenant with the church, thus rendering territorial promises as entirely redundant. For Christian Zionists, replacement is tantamount to apostasy, as well as being antisemitic of course. It denies the unique covenant God made with ethnic Israel. And because replacement is such a serious sin—which it is, if by replacement we mean a kind of Marcionite rejection of anything before Christ—in my experience one only needs to dally with the idea, or say something that skirts close to the idea of replacement, to be guilty of it. On one occasion, for example, in my early years at Millmead, I made a comment in a sermon suggesting that Jesus changing water into wine in Cana of Galilee had some kind of spiritual significance beyond just the miracle, and was possibly a critique of the ceremonial law of Judaism. Go to any reputable commentary on John's Gospel, such as C. K. Barrett, or Don Carson, and you will find exactly this angle. Nothing particularly controversial there.[9] But interpreted through the lens of some in the congregation that morning, I may as well have denied the deity of Christ, such was their outrage. As far they were concerned, to challenge even aspects of the ancient covenant with Israel—in this instance a routine comment about first-century

9. It just so happens that I am revisiting this part of my argument on the feast day of Bishop Westcott, one of the finest Anglican New Testament scholars. In his commentary on this passage, which I have just taken down from the shelf here in the library at Chichester Cathedral, we read this: "In each respect the character of the sign answers to the general character of Christ as a new creation, a transfiguration of the ceremonial Law into a spiritual Gospel, the ennobling of the whole of life." Westcott, *Gospel according to John*, 39.

Judaism—is to challenge the whole, and put oneself in a peril-
ous place, since to speak against Israel is to speak against God.
Indeed, it is hard to think of more emotive reactions than those
of Christian Zionists. Worship elicits strong feelings, to be sure,
and neo-Pentecostals can get heated about baptism in the Spirit.
But in my experience it is nothing compared to the controversy
engendered by the suspicion of replacement theology. As we saw
earlier, the emotions are visceral, highly personal, and sometimes
irrational—more so even than right-wing Zionism, which at least
must submit itself to the democratic process.

The Heady Days of Christian Zionism

As I look back at that at that period, and as I observe things at present among fundamentalists, it takes some time to work out why
Christian Zionism emerged as such a strong force, and why it retains such appeal now. Historically, it finds its antecedents in Puri-
tan millenarianism, as well as nineteenth-century Restorationism.[10]
If you want evidence of how passionately some nineteenth-century
evangelicals believed in the conversion of the Jews as a prelude to
the return of Christ, make a visit to the remarkable chapel of St.
Paul which was rebuilt in 1804 by Lewis Way, the then incumbent
of Stansted House in West Sussex. The Jewish iconography in the
east window above the altar, as well as the Hebrew texts, are a
most strange sight, to be sure, and not particularly attractive, in
my opinion. But the chapel reminds us that Christian Zionism was
espoused at the very highest echelons of British society.[11] The cause

10. For a useful and surprisingly non-partisan overview of the historical and theological roots of Christian Zionism, see Sizer, *Christian Zionism*,
26–105.

11. As Munro Price recounts, Lewis Way cultivated a most unlikely relationship with Alexander I, the Russian Tsar, who likewise believed history was
approaching its apocalyptic destiny. Way also counted among his acquaintanc-
es the eccentric Lady Hestor Stanhope. From these connections Price is able
to draw a line from Lewis Way to the millenarianism of Edward Irving, the
dispensationalism of John Nelson Darby, and the apocalypticism of Hal Lindsey in the twentieth century. Price and Price, *Road to the Apocalypse*, 111–17.

was taken up mid-century by Lord Ashley, who later became the Earl of Shaftesbury. And then of course there is the Balfour declaration at the beginning of the twentieth. The reasons why the British government made this promise in 1917 to assist in the creation of a Jewish homeland are numerous and complex. It would be disingenuous to say that it was all religiously motivated. Nevertheless, it is well known that many of the architects of this landmark piece— Arthur Balfour and David Lloyd George—were devout Christians who knew the topography of the Holy Land as well as they did their own country.[12] To assist in the return of the Jews to the land of Israel had a feel of God's providence about it.

Why Christian Zionism reemerged as such a strong movement in the latter part of the twentieth century, both here and in the United States, is a result, in my estimation, of several cultural factors: the rise of religious fundamentalism in general; the ascendency of right-wing ideologies; and the growing nervousness around end of the century apocalyptic. The attractiveness for the Protestant wing of the Christian community of a theology that offered biblical certainties (and territorial ones at that) in a time of growing uncertainty cannot be overstated. To have tangible evidence of God's actions in the world, when in every other respect the church was adrift in "a sea of faith," was no small thing, and explains why a literalistic premillennial dispensationalism, which is perhaps the most dominant form of Christian Zionism, enjoyed such a resurgence—and why it has survived to this day. Millenarianism may have died down a little since the turn of the century, but radical secularism hasn't. If anything, it has intensified. Hence, to have clear and tangible evidence of God's purpose in the world is not only convenient but pastorally comforting. Christian Zionism provides for its supporters a rare opportunity of prophetic credibility: the War of Independence; the euphoria of the Six-Day War in 1967, which included significant territorial gains; the subsequent rise in immigration to Israel, especially from the Soviet Union; the Yom Kippur War of 1973; and Jewish settlements on the West Bank were all regarded as an attestation

12. See Hamilton, *God, Guns and Israel*, 14–15.

7

of biblical prophecy and offered a trajectory of triumph that was compelling. The dramatic capture of East Jerusalem in 1967, which allowed access to the Western Wall, had all the hallmarks of end-time prophecy, and fitted the narrative perfectly. Pictures of Moshe Dayan with young Israeli soldiers standing at the Kotel was the stuff of dreams.[13]

The fact that political Zionism was a secular movement, and that Israel's growing tourist industry was as much focused on hedonism as it was on holy sites, is beside the point. Christian Zionism possessed a seemingly incontrovertible drama that organizations like ICEJ amplified to the full. I recall turning up to a meeting at the Christian Embassy in the summer of 1983 and hearing the director, Jan Willem van der Hoeven, speak about Jerusalem as the "eternal, indivisible capital of the Jewish state." He was bound to say that. The promotion of a reunited city was, after all, the rationale for the creation of the Christian Embassy in Jerusalem in response to the withdrawal to Tel Aviv of the last remaining foreign embassies. Even so, the speech was delivered with prophetic passion. For a young nineteen-year-old charismatic evangelical, who spent most of that summer devouring the Old Testament, it was intoxicating. The fact that the son of one of my host families was fighting in the Lebanon only added to the drama.[14]

The early eighties were heady days for Christian Zionism in yet another way, namely the steady arrival of Ethiopian Jews in the country. Operation Solomon, which successfully evacuated just over a thousand Falasha (as they were known) from Addis Ababa

13. Michael Northcott notes that the Six Day War of 1967 presaged the publication of Hal Lindsey's *The Late Great Planet Earth*, whose recasting of dispensationalism around the current affairs in the latter half of the twentieth century helped turn dispensationalism from a fringe theology into a mainstream conviction among American evangelicals. Northcott, *Angel Directs the Storm*, 62–63.

14. His sister had already completed her national service and would eventually do important archive work, so I discovered, at Sde Boker, Ben-Gurion's home in the Negev. I remain to this day deeply indebted to them, and their dear mother who adopted me as her "Christian" son. For the most recent biography of Ben-Gurion, much of which is based on archive materials from Sde Boker, see Segev, *State at Any Cost*.

airport to Tel Aviv, was still a decade away. But for many Christian Zionists the discovery of this lost tribe, and their aliyah to Eretz Israel, added to the excitement of that time. I lived alongside several of them in an Absorption Centre in Ashkelon. The object of the exercise was for us to experience, for at least a month, the process by which new arrivals entered the country. For many people it is in fact a challenging experience. Many don't make it, ending up returning to the country they came from. But when you are in pursuit of a vision, those statistics don't really count. They didn't matter for me at the time. For myself, the sight of Ethiopian Jews walking up and down the corridors where we lived, coupled to the sound of Russian Jews singing on Shabbat in the synagogue just across the way, was truly romantic. I may feel differently these days about the ideology of Christian Zionism, but I cannot deny, nor want to deny, the fascination I felt. By any standard, the return of Jews to Israel is a phenomenal piece of history. It is understandable why some Christians interpret this return in the way they do.

To be fair to many of the Christian Zionists I knew at the time, not all were uncritical of Israel. Just because they stood in solidarity with the country, and had a vision of restoration, does not mean they condoned all the actions of the Israeli Government. My arrival in Israel was only a few months after the Sabra and Shatila massacre in Lebanon, carried out by the Christian Phalange. Apart from those extremist voices, who to this day condone anything that the Israeli government does, several Christian Zionists that I knew joined in the condemnation of the IDF who were charged with standing-by while the massacre took place. No matter that Ariel Sharon was popular among Christian evangelicals as a kind of biblical figure; his resignation as defense secretary in the aftermath of the massacre was regarded by many people as entirely appropriate.

The same discernment is exercised these days over a whole range of issues, from checkpoints, to the use of tear gas, to even the matter of settlements. Not all Christian Zionists are comfortable with the present situation. Nevertheless, for all the nuance, one cannot help thinking that their solidarity with Israel prevents a full and proper critique of her actions. In any other context we would be quick, as believers in Christ, to name aggression or discrimination for what it is; but when it comes to Israel, we seem to make excuses—sometimes because our support is blind, or sometimes out of fear of antisemitism. Many Christian Zionists, as well as many of my Jewish friends, point out the hypocrisy the other way. They accuse the media of double standards and a stringency towards Israel that simply does not apply to other nations. While I can certainly sympathize with that and acknowledge the unique history that makes Israel so incredibly vulnerable, it is precisely the uniqueness of Israel's vocation that exacts higher standards from her. Indeed, it was my growing conviction about the responsibilities that ought to attend any theology of exceptionalism—including our own exceptionalism—that caused my eyes to open to the plight of the Palestinians which hitherto I had managed to ignore. That I then started to devour revisionist histories of Israel is what happens when you fall out of love. More on that later. Suffice to say, I was beginning to see that the situation was more complex than Christian Zionism made out, although none more complex than the sensitivities around the Holocaust. It is to this aspect of the politics and theology that I should now like to turn.

Holocaust Reckoning

It just so happened that my first few months in Israel coincided with Holocaust Memorial Day. Sirens go off around the country to mark the occasion. In the school I was teaching, the day was handed over to lessons and assemblies, all seeking to inculcate in the next generation the horrors of Shoah, which is also, in many ways, the rationale for the country. After all, it was the grim reality of six million Jewish deaths at the hands of the Nazis that provided the impetus for the UN resolution to grant the Jewish people their own homeland.

The interwar dictatorships, including Fascist antisemitism in Nazi Germany, is a subject I went on to teach in the late eighties at an independent Grammar School in Kingston, London. One of my students was the writer Tanya Gold, whose mother, Trudy, I recall, had recently joined the Spiro Institute for the Study of Jewish History and Culture. I met her a few times at parents' evenings and was deeply impressed by her commitment to establish the teaching of Shoah in the British curriculum. A few years earlier, during my time as an undergraduate at Durham University, I had already formed a friendship with Melissa Raphael, who went on to write one of the most remarkable books on the Holocaust. *The Female Face of God in Auschwitz* is not only research of the highest order but quite the most stunning theodicy, in which Professor Raphael argues for the presence of God in Auschwitz through the tender gestures of Jewish women caring for one another.[15]

None of this qualifies me to speak about this subject, but it does at least indicate a passion to engage with it. The literature is extensive and the memorials compelling.[16] One of the most haunting buildings I have ever seen is the great synagogue in Oradea, Romania. Now boarded up and padlocked, it was the pride of one of the biggest Jewish communities in the country, many of whom died in the concentration camps. For a while, not long after I arrived at Millmead, I was teaching one week every year at Emanuel University in Oradea. I would never fail to pay my respects to the place. These days the Jewish community is no more than three thousand people, and the synagogue is simply a relic. But like so many of these synagogues, it is testament to a very deep wound in European history. I have never been to Auschwitz. I am told it is a devastating experience. But empty synagogues are, in perhaps a more elegiac way, a similarly devastating sight.

In Israel there are numerous memorials. Yad Vashem is often regarded as the most shocking as well as the most curious since it also includes The Avenue of the Righteous Among the Nations. As a new Christian, I was anxious to see the tree planted for Corrie ten Boom, a Dutch believer whose family had harbored Jews in their house, and whose story had attained

---

15. Raphael, *Female Face of God in Auschwitz*.

16. For compelling primary sources in the extensive Holocaust literature, see Hillesum, *Interrupted Life*; Wiesel, *Night*; Levi, *If This Is a Man and Truce*.

something like legendary status among evangelicals. In later years I became aware, as we all did on account of the award-winning film *Schindler's List*, that Oscar Schindler also had a tree planted there in his name. On this most recent visit to Israel, forty years to the month since my first visit, I came across his grave in a cemetery just south of Mount Zion. Not surprisingly, it had all the marks of being a place of pilgrimage, such as a small cairn of stones by the headstone. As a mark of my own respect, I added a stone and paused for a few moments of silence, remembering not only the courage of this rather unlikely hero, but also the many others who risked their lives to save Jewish people.[17]

The relationship between the Holocaust and the state of Israel is, at one level, very straightforward. Historically, it is not difficult to demonstrate a direct link between antisemitism in Europe and the growing clamor among Zionists for a homeland so that "never again" would world Jewry be subjected to such crimes. Zionism predates the Holocaust, by a long way. This is worth remembering. Its antecedents lie elsewhere, although not unrelated to the matter of persecution, especially in Russia. But it was undoubtedly the Holocaust that provided the sense of urgency. As the novelist Chaim Potok depicts in his classic novel *The Chosen*, the UN vote for a Jewish State is set against the horror of genocide in Europe. The campaigning of Rabbi Malter for the Zionist cause among American Jews is one of the main subplots of the novel.[18] What the novel also depicts, however, is the strain that his Zionism places on the unlikely friendship between his son Reuven and Daniel Saunders, the son of the ultraorthodox Reb Saunders. As much as the Rebbe is likewise devastated by the news emerging from Europe—the all-too-familiar hatred of his people—he cannot possibly subscribe to the notion of a secular Jewish state and forbids Daniel to have any contact with Reuven. Once the State of Israel becomes a reality, the friendship

17. One of the most inspiring stories of rescue emerges from the French mountain village of Le Chambon-sur-Lignon, where a pacifist Huguenot community sheltered three thousand Jewish children from the searching antisemitism of the Vichy government. For a good introduction to the story, see Moorhead, *The Village of Secrets*. See also Grose, *Greatest Escape*.

18. Potok, *Chosen*.

is allowed to resume since it can no longer be a point of dissension. But what the novel demonstrates is the complexity of the matter. The Holocaust is what it is: a story of clinical evil—evil precisely because it is so clinical. What is not so clear are the political and theological ramifications of such evil, including the place that the Holocaust should have in the collective psyche of a nation.

As a Christian one must tread carefully here. We are hardly qualified to speak on the matter. The last thing we should be doing is opening up further the fissures that exist between Christians and Jews. If anything, we should be seeking rapprochement. But what I note is a nervousness within Judaism itself about this issue. As the late Jonathan Sacks points out in *Future Tense: A Vision for Jews and Judaism in the Global Culture*, if Zionism is to be a transformative and hopeful agent in the world, and true therefore to its original vocation, then it must become more than the sum of its enemies. This is not to deny the tragedy of its history; but rather to make sure that hope triumphs over it. Otherwise, says Rabbi Sacks, Jews will simply end up as the victims, and if there is any psychology that is more damaging to the human soul it is the mentality of the victim. I know this as a pastor. When a person adopts the mindset of the victim, they are almost impossible to reach. Indeed, their perception of themselves as isolated and alone becomes a self-fulfilling prophecy. How much more so in matters of statecraft.

If we define ourselves by our enemies, says Rabbi Sacks, then isolationism quickly follows. Zionism ceases to be a hopeful vision of the future, but a depressing retreat into sectarianism. Whether modern Israel is guilty of this mindset is not really for me to comment. I have observed it, just as I have observed the opposite, not least in the generosity of people like Jonathan Sacks. Where I do feel compelled to comment is when this siege mentality is fuelled by Christian Zionists who, without any personal experience of Judaism's troubled history, often go beyond even the far right in demonizing the enemy. To be fair, this is often done in the interests of solidarity. The existential threat that Israel still faces, despite over seventy years of independence, is a real one. But the solidarity can be overdone, if that doesn't sound like a contradiction in terms, to the point where Christian Zionism is sometimes more Zionist than Zionism, if that makes sense.[19] Whether out of collective guilt, or sheer wilfulness, the darkness of the Holocaust can so dominate Christian thinking about Israel that it falls prey to the very mindset that Rabbi Sacks exhorts the Jewish community to avoid.

It doesn't have to be that way. It is entirely possible to support Israel in the global context without evoking images of the camps, just as it is entirely possible to support Israel without resorting to messianism. Indeed, the Christian Council on Palestine, founded in 1942 by Reinhold Niebuhr, was an explicit rejection of messianic ideology in favor of a straightforward moral approach to the search for a homeland for the Jews. It was only with the capture of East Jerusalem in the Six-Day War that Christian propheticism began to take over. And within that end-time vision of a restored Israel, it is undoubtedly the case that the Holocaust has acted as something of an apocalyptic. In a sense, how could it be otherwise? The extermination of six million Jews is, by every indicator, apocalyptic, and every attempt should be made to remember it. Holocaust memorial days should become more important as time passes, not less. But Rabbi Sacks is right: how that memory is traditioned, how central it becomes to the overall narrative of a Jewish people, and how it therefore shapes attitudes towards the other, is critical for the future of Judaism in a global culture. One wonders if Christian Zionism is a help or a hindrance in this regard. By propagating its own version of what Sacks calls "a people that dwell alone" myth, supported by an idiosyncratic biblical hermeneutic, the irony is that Christian Zionism could perpetuate the very mindset that Sacks and others would like Jews to jettison. As he concludes in *Future Tense*:

---

19. "More Zionist than Zionism" is a phrase I was going to use as a title for the book, until I discovered that the term had already been used in an article in the *Washington Post* by William Claiborne entitled "America's Evangelicals: More Zionist than Zionism." Quoted in Chapman, *Whose Promised Land?*, 206–7.

Israel must prevail over its fears, and not see every criticism as a form of antisemitism or Jewish self-hatred. Jews must stop seeing themselves as victims. They should remember that the word "chosen" means that Jews are called on to be self-critical, never forgetting the tasks they have been set and have not yet completed.[20]

As with so much that Sacks has written, there is profound wisdom here, as well as courage. I was so taken with his understanding of what the word "chosen" implies, I decided to try it out on some Christians who I knew to be strongly pro-Israel, hoping it would ameliorate some of their attitudes. I was wrong. They dismissed it as misguided, and even challenged Rabbi Sack's credentials to speak on the matter, thus confirming the very thing that he was highlighting, namely the pathology that develops when one is unwilling to self-critique. The Holocaust is gargantuan, sure enough. It is *sui generis*. Very few weeks pass by when one is not confronted, even now, by the legacy of this unspeakable atrocity. But, as Sacks warns, to stay in that memory is precarious, even as it might be essential. As shocking as it sounds, it is entirely possible in any trauma for the abused to end up as the abuser.

According to journalist Thomas Friedman, this is precisely what happened with Menachem Begin, prime minister of Israel from 1977 to 1983. Given the fact that both his parents and his elder brother Herzl were murdered in the Holocaust, it was impossible for Begin to view the Arabs as anything other than Nazis in disguise. Begin believed, argues Friedman, that the siege of Arafat's forces was the moral equivalent of going after "Hitler in his bunker."[21] Even after years of military success, tanks, jets and bombs became "his pornography," the cure for Jewish impotence. What made Begin so dangerous, if not reckless—and there is no doubt that Israeli politics took a decisive change in the late seventies—is that he never ceased to see himself as a victim. This may not excuse Begin's extreme politics, but it may well explain it. We may even want to forgive it. What is less easy to forgive, and difficult to explain, however, is when this

20. Sacks, *Future Tense*, 261.

21. Friedman, *From Beirut to Jerusalem*, 143–44.

same pathology carries over into the next generation, or when the same tropes are perpetuated as a way of avoiding the risky and painful business of peace-making.

For me, Benjamin Netanyahu's handling of the Oslo Peace Accords is a good example of this kind of thing. Caught out by the secrecy of the talks between Yitzhak Rabin and Yasser Arafat, and no doubt seeking to make maximum political gain for Likud, he likened Oslo to Chamberlain's famous "Peace in our Time" promise which he brought back from Munich.[22] This was no throwaway line, but a deeply embedded psychology residing in someone who should have known better—a stereotype that simply reinforces the cycle of violence. In his defense, his comments were made in the context of multiple suicide bombings in Israel—a clear attempt by terrorists to destabilize the peace process. But what Netanyahu's comments perpetuate is something which all fundamentalist ideologies are prone to, including Christian Zionism, which is the demonization of the enemy.

I would like to think that the Jesus ethic of nonviolence, which includes loving one's enemies, would counter this, just as I know that many Israelis work hard to overcome these stereotypes by befriending actual Palestinians. But my own experience among Christian Zionists, at least to date, has been equivocal. For all the attempts to understand the conflict, and to sympathize with the Arab situation, there is something about the way Christian Zionism sets up the drama that makes it vulnerable to these tired but oftentimes dangerous stereotypes. We do it as Brits of course. It doesn't take much, as I discovered when teaching interwar dictatorships in secondary school, to cast all Germans as Nazis. It is not something that has been outlawed yet by the politically correct censors. But that doesn't mean to say we should encourage it. As Rabbi Sacks reminds us, there are tasks we have been set, and which have yet to be completed.

---

22. Pfeffer, *Bibi*, 292.

Beyond Christian Zionism

Trying to recall one's feelings forty years on is, I imagine, a challenging task for anyone trying to write a memoir. To retrieve one's idealism—let's call it fundamentalism—as a nineteen-year-old, when so much has changed, is always going to be difficult, if not traumatic. On my most recent visit to Jerusalem, literally forty years to the month since I first arrived, I happened to be staying at St. Andrew's Hostel, which is right next to the new Menachem Begin Heritage Centre. Although I didn't go round the exhibition, simply walking past it each morning on my way up to the Jaffa Gate triggered so many memories of the early eighties when my evangelicalism was so wedded to his expansionist agenda. I don't believe I had anything like Jerusalem syndrome. That is a psychotic illness, and not pleasant to observe. But I do think I was in a bit of a whirl. In the eighties, Zionism was in the air. Everywhere I went, everything I heard, seemed to confirm the end-time vision.

The irony of the situation is that I had no intention of going to Israel at the beginning of 1983. I was working in a Leonard Cheshire home for the first few months of my gap year and was looking to head out to India. Only last minute did the opportunity to go to Israel come up. Hence, the fact I returned from Israel in the summer as an ardent Christian Zionist has a certain comedy about it. I don't regret it. Dare I say, I see something providential about it. I would not have understood the strength of feelings I encountered a couple of decades later. But even so, it was a bit wild. As with anyone who emerges from what I can only describe as Christian fundamentalism, I look back with a certain degree of incredulity. There is both frustration as well as affection.

The affection relates to the fact that I admire anyone who has passion. Better to be passionate than indifferent. The frustration, however, relates to the sheer intransigence of the people who hold those ideas. I experience the same these days with the progressive left. Social Justice Warriors, so-called, can be some of the most impossible people you will ever meet. Their ideology is unforgiving. Like all utopians, they think nothing of stringing up their enemies—even their friends. Indeed, they make a virtue of it. But what bothers me now, as I recall my own dalliance with conservative fundamentalism in the early eighties, is that some of that terrifying virtue is beginning to reemerge, particularly in the United States. Christian Zionism in the UK seems to be a bit of a spent force. It certainly doesn't have the appeal or proponents that it had in the eighties. In the States, however, it seems to be as strong as ever. President Biden may express his concern about right-wing extremism in Israel, but it is a brave president who will take that to the ballot box. More politically astute, it pains me to say, was Donald Trump's recognition in 2017 of Jerusalem as the capital of Israel. Along with his anti-abortion stance, it confirmed him, bizarrely, as the darling of the evangelical right.

At what point I began my own journey away from that kind of ideology is hard to say. As is often the case, it was gradual rather than a moment in time. Indeed, I can recall a visit in the summer of 1988 to a religious moshav, near to the Dead Sea, and being deeply impressed by the people I met, even as I was trying to distance myself from the ideology they held. It's complicated. For sure, I can remember defining moments, and in part two I shall try to recount them. They relate to my first real experience of the Palestinian problem, as well as a rethink on biblical hermeneutics. But at what point I permitted myself to think differently is hard to say.

Part of the difficulty remembering is that I never lost my interest in all things Jewish. At the same time as I was having misgivings about Christian Zionism, I was strengthening my appreciation of Jewish culture and religion. I read through all of Chaim Potok's novels; got fascinated by Hasidic spirituality; developed a love of Chagall; and never stopped learning about Jewish history. Like many Christians, I felt at home in the world of Judaism in a way that I could never feel at home in the world of Islam or Hinduism. Even though there had been a parting of the ways between Jews and Christians, and not a little acrimony, we were still cousins. Christian Zionism, on the other hand, was a different animal. It was different even to Zionism. So even as my reading became more Jewish, or maybe because my reading became more Jewish, my faith became less enamored with the rarefied world of Christian Zionism.

One thing I do recall, which has a kind of prescience about it, is hearing David Pawson give a series of sermons in 1988 on the theme of the return of Christ. I had never heard David preach, nor had any idea that I would eventually, about fifteen years later, lead the congregation that he founded at Millmead. All I knew is that he was in great demand as a speaker, was a good friend of Andrew Gilmour, who owned the Christian bookshop in Staines, and was willing to come, at the request of his friend, to speak to our gathering. At the end of the three nights, there was hardly a person who wasn't in awe at what David shared. It too was in awe. As always, his speaking was mesmerizing. But I found myself disagreeing with him on just about every point he made. The biggest problem I had was his failure to contextualize Jesus's apocalyptic speeches. The idea that some of Jesus's warnings might relate more accurately to the imminent destruction of Jerusalem by the Romans hardly featured at all in David's reckoning. Everything was to do with the end-times, and end-times of course meant the return of the Jews to the land of Israel. I do remember him talking about that.

At the time, I didn't have the theological tools to articulate what I felt. It was more an instinct. But I knew enough to know that the genre of apocalyptic required careful handling and deserved more than a simple "this is that" kind of exegesis. David knew this too of course. As a bible preacher, routinely preaching the word of God, he was always strong on context. I once heard him give an outstanding lecture to a company of preachers about the historical background to the Song of Songs. To this day, I draw upon it. But when it came to single issues that he felt strongly about—which is what he spent a great deal of his time promoting once he left Millmead—those disciplines seemed to disappear. He was literal, dogmatic, and quite imposing.[23]

---

23. Northcott notes the difference between contemporary scholarship and popular fundamentalism concerning the focus of Jesus's apocalyptic. Northcott, *Angel Directs the Storm*, 64–65.

I realized then, though I had no idea how poignant it would prove to be, that I had moved on in my thinking about Israel. The reason I was unable to espouse Christian Zionism at Millmead, so many years later, and watched so many people leave the church over it, was because I had come to regarded it, many years before, as literal-minded fundamentalism. I loved Israel, and as an evangelical I was passionate about spreading the gospel. I still am. I am passionate about preaching the gospel to the Jews. I would regard as it as antisemitic not to. After all, the gospel of salvation that St. Paul heralds is "first to the Jew, then to the gentile."[24] What I was finding increasingly hard to uphold, however, all those years ago, was a theology, in the form of Christian Zionism, that took that simple gospel imperative and turned it into a scheme.

It has occurred to me, over the years, that maybe I am just averse to apocalyptic, and that this explains why I distanced myself from Christian Zionism in the way I did. Possibly so. I confess that I don't feel entirely at home in the world of Daniel, for example, or Revelation. Who does? What I prefer to believe, however, is that I am averse not to apocalyptic, as such, but to a particular kind of apocalyptic: one that fosters not only a highly idiosyncratic view of the Scriptures, but also an attitude among its followers that is polemical, political and just a little bit paranoid. Nothing has transpired in my conversations over the years with Christian Zionists to dissuade me from this opinion. I suspect that whatever happens in Arab-Israeli politics in the next chapter, Christian Zionism will find a way to accommodate it to their vision. It would be impossible for them to not do so. Notwithstanding the greater sophistication that exists among this present generation of Christian Zionists, it's not long into a conversation that one encounters the same intransigence. I call it polemical. We might also call it a kind of laziness: an unwillingness to wrestle with complex theological horizons and painful political realities. It is these two things that I should like to now consider.

24. Rom 1:16.

Part Two

A New Hermeneutic

Revisiting Palestine

IN THE SUMMER OF 2010, as a matter of routine, I booked a medical. As a church, we had a deal with an agency called Interserve, so as the minister I availed myself of the opportunity to have a free checkup at one of their centers in London. Strangely, along with the booking, I received a complimentary ticket to see a play at the Young Vic, which was just round the corner from where I had the medical. Not wanting to turn down a freebee, I decided to go.

The play was called *I Am Yusuf and This Is My Brother*, by Amir Nizar Zuabi, about the plight of three Palestinian communities during the last years of the British mandate.[1] The dialogue was beautiful, as I recall—not political so much as poetic, a kind of lament for lost communities both prior to and during the war that inevitably followed the British withdrawal from Palestine. In fact, the play is as much a critique of British mishandling as it is of Jewish aggression. Given it was a Palestinian theater troupe, I do remember feeling uncomfortable in one or two scenes.

The scene that haunts me most, however, and at the time brought me to tears, is when an old man enters the stage carrying

1. Zuabi, *I Am Yusuf and This Is My Brother*.

an uprooted tree on this back. At one level it is quite comedic, but very soon it takes on the tone of the tragic because of course this is a tree he had planted, and from which he will not be parted despite the forced removal from his village. Rather than describe the scene any further, let me give you some of the dialogue:

> Man: You! Will you help me?
>
> Yusuf: Yes, Uncle.
>
> Ali: Why?
>
> Man: What?
>
> Ali: Why the tree?
>
> Man: I planted this tree seven years ago. For four years it was too young to bear fruit. A cold winter came, it almost died and took a full year to recover. Then, fruit. My neighbour's children picked it, all of it, long before it was ripe. This tree I have been tending for some time now and only last year did I taste its fruit.
>
> Ali: It's a sin to uproot a healthy tree!
>
> Man: What happens to me will happen to it. That became clear as I walked out of my house, so I went back and dug it up.
>
> Ali: You'll kill it or it will kill you. Look at the state you're in.
>
> Man: I left my house. I left my land, I left my hills, I left my well in the Ibn Amer valley. Where am I going? I've no idea. I'm fifty and I've never once left my valley. Why would I? But now, now I am going to the plains and the dust. I won't leave my tree. I won't become a small ring in a big trunk.

I Am Yusuf and This Is My Brother was something of an awakening for me. I felt like the writer and liberation theologian Kelley Nikondeha when she read Thomas Friedman's bestseller, *From Beirut to Jerusalem*, for the first time. "This prompted an epiphany for me," she writes. "Nowhere in my Christian tradition was the story of the Palestinian people told. Now I was confronted with the reality of the Palestinians living in the same territory I'd studied the Scriptures my entire life. I saw clearly for the first time a history that had been intentionally hidden."[2]

My own experience may not have been as painful as Kelley's. She says that the memory of that epiphany still stings. Nevertheless, my exposure to *I Am Yusuf* certainly opened me up to a very different narrative, and eventually a very different historiography, as a result of which I was able to view the Palestinian people through the lens of their suffering rather than the terrorism which, among Christians Zionists at least, was so much the dominant image of Palestinian identity. The play allowed me to feel the immense grief that lies just below the surface of this displaced people. For the Palestinians, the War of Independence, as it is referred to in Israel and commemorated every May 14, is nothing less than a catastrophe—the *Nakba*, as it is called in Arabic.

As is often the case when you wake to a different story, I read everything I could get my hands on, and swung the pendulum of my convictions to completely the other extreme. As a historian, I had always been open to revisionist histories. My very first published article was a survey of the revisionist approach to the English Reformation. Revisionism in the Arab-Israeli context, however, is far more provocative, and what is particularly notable about much of the literature is that it is written by Israeli historians. It just so happens that the editor for one these histories, *The Ethnic Cleansing of Palestine*, by Illan Pappe, was also the editor for of one my own books. But whereas my book is an innovative but fairly noncontroversial reflection on matters of spirituality, Pappe's book is nothing short of scandalous. It is borderline libellous, and had the referencing not been so precise I imagine it would have been charged as such. What made the book so disturbing to read was not just the unfamiliarity of a counter narrative (which is always unsettling) but also the fact that the book did resonate with some of my own, albeit limited experiences of life in Israel: all the way from relatively isolated incidents of racism against Arab migrant workers which I witnessed on the

2. Nikondeha, *First Advent in Palestine*, 18–19.

kibbutz, to something even more sinister—what Pappe refers to as the memoricide of Arab settlements.

Memoricide is a provocative term, to be sure. In the context of Israel's history, it refers to the deliberate erasure of Arab culture, and the examples Pappe cites include the Palestinian town of Al-Majdal.[3] At the time of the 1948 Arab-Israeli war, Al-Majdal had a Christian-Muslim population of 10,000, but when it was conquered by Israeli forces on November 5, 1948, much of the town fled. Today the town of Ashkelon is almost entirely Jewish. I know that because I lived there for a while. Such was the effectiveness of memoricide—which included, under the instructions of Moshe Dayan, the demolition in 1950 of an eleventh-century mosque—it was only years later, in conversation with someone from the exchange program, that I realized that Majdal had even existed. As far as I was concerned, Ashkelon was settled in the 1950s by South African Jews. That there used to be a thriving Arab community in the vicinity, based on the woollen industry, was simply not part of the narrative I had received. We had plenty of orientation activities in the first week of our stay, including a very irreverent parody of the Christmas story by the program leader, but nothing at all was said about the Palestinian past.

Whether my ignorance of Majdal can be attributable to attempts at memoricide is, of course, wide open to debate. Memoricide is an emotive term and a politicized take on what may simply be cultural erosion. As someone who is half Welsh, I do know a bit about this. I am still open to that possibility. As far as Pappe is concerned, however, my lack of awareness was precisely a result of memoricide; and how this was achieved was very intentional on the part of Israel's architects, none more so than the rather sinister practice of forestation. The aim of this program, which according to Pappe was widespread in the early years following independence, was to erase every trace of previous settlement and through the introduction of conifers, for example, create a far more European landscape.[4]

3. Pappe, *Ethnic Cleansing of Palestine*, 227.

4. Interestingly, Simon Schama begins his monumental book *Landscape*

On all my visits to Israel, I am not sure I would describe the fauna as particularly European. I don't know enough about trees to discern the nuance. Nor have I ever seen the rather spooky reappearance of olive trees which, in one instance, according to Pappe, split a considerably less robust pine tree in half. But what I was subjected to, time and again from the Israelis I met, both in the early eighties, and then in the late eighties when I traveled with my wife, Susanna, was the classic refrain, so central to the mythology of Christian Zionism, that there was nothing there by way of culture and cultivation before the Zionists arrived. That's called memoricide.

An interesting feature of this myth concerns the occurrence of malaria which, ironically, there is some historical evidence of. In describing the settlement of socialist kibbutzniks in the Harod Valley in the early 1920s, Ari Shavit is methodical in chronicling their success in reclaiming the land from the deadly marshes in which the Anopheles mosquitos bred.[5] But whereas propagandists have used this to political effect, implying that the land was an un-cultivated backwater of the Ottoman empire, Shavit is at pains to honor the indigenous communities that existed before the arrival of Jewish settlements. His very personal, almost elegiac story of some of the most pivotal moments in Israel's history confirms that the Arab communities which fled because of the war of 1948 were indeed historic, deeply embedded, and culturally rich. The irony, from a Christian Zionist point of view, is that a significant number of these Arab populations were also Christian.

---

and Memory with a delightful story from his childhood about gumming small green leaves to a paper tree, pinned to the wall of his *cheder*, the proceeds of which went to the planting of pine trees in Israel. See Schama, *Landscape and Memory*, 5–6. Given Schama's antipathy to John Berger's call in 2006 for an academic boycott of Israel, one can only imagine his disdain for the work of Illan Pappe. Of Berger's Open Letter, which was signed by ninety-two other leading artists, Schama wrote: "This is not the first boycott call directed at Jews. On 1 April 1933, one week after he came to power, Hitler ordered a boycott of Jewish shops, banks, offices and department stores." See Schama and Julias, "John Berger Is Wrong."

5. See Shavit, *My Promised Land*, 25–47.

In terms of my journey away from Christian Zionism, Pappe's work was significant. Just as I swallowed the Zionist myth whole as a young impressionable nineteen-year-old—including the oft-quoted refrain: "a land without a people for a people without a land"—I likewise swallowed Pappe whole, and for a while took up the Palestinian cause with an almost political fervor. I registered the injustices of this displaced people with something approaching righteous indignation. There is no one more fanatical than a new convert. These days I regard the situation as far more complex than goodies and baddies, whichever way you go on the issue. Regarding Pappe, I should like to make it clear that I now regard much of his work as polemic. I am more inclined to the view of celebrated writer Amos Oz that this is not a conflict of right or wrong. This is a case of two people groups who both have legitimate claims. As he states at the beginning of *How to Cure a Fanatic*, which like much of his work is an attempt to charter a more pragmatic approach:

> The Israeli-Palestinian conflict is not a Wild West movie. It is not a struggle between good and evil, rather it is a tragedy in the ancient and most precise sense of the word: a clash between right and right, and clash between one very powerful, deep and convincing claim and another very different but no less convincing, no less powerful, no less humane claim.[6]

As a campaigner for peace, Oz's comments are wise. His famous dictum "Make Peace, not Love" is a timely reminder that a two-state solution—if that is still a possibility—doesn't have to be accompanied by gushy sentiments but by political realism. As a Christian, I may aspire to something more radical in terms of loving one's enemies, but in terms of *realpolitik* an amicable divorce may well be a more achievable. After all, as Oz points out, these are two people with two competing narratives. The historiographies that accompany those narratives have become a battleground itself. These days we not only have revisionist histories,

---

6. Oz, *How to Cure a Fanatic*, 4–5. See also Oz, *Dear Zealots*. For a most poignant childhood memory of growing up in the Yishuv, see also Oz, *Tale of Love and Darkness*.

but counter-revisionist histories from the old historians, who turn out of course to be the new historians.[7] So rather than arguing the toss as to who has the correct version, maybe it is simply time to concede that both sides have a case.[8] Just so. But since my own starting point was more aligned to Israel, and since Christian Zionism is the theology that has continued to impinge on the churches I have served, then I do feel an obligation, as Rabbi Sacks urges, to at least be open to the hard work of self-critique. Any group that claims chosen status—and there is no group more convinced of their chosen status than Christian Zionists—should also shoulder the burden of responsibility, lest their privileges end up as presumptions. It is incumbent upon them to read not just the stories of Jewish persecution, of which there are many, or Arab atrocities, which are not difficult to summon, but also the stories which describe Palestinian suffering. By attending to this, by suspending for a moment the notion, as I mentioned earlier, of moral equivalence, and seeking instead to truly understand the grievances that lie on the other side of the divide, maybe it is not too late for some progress to be made. It is unlikely, to be sure, but that doesn't mean it shouldn't be attempted.

In my naivety, I do in fact believe that the Christian community has some role to play here. Further, I also believe that the UK church has a role to play, not because we are a moral arbiter—we relinquished that reputation long ago when we gave up the Mandate—but simply because we have historic, spiritual and emotional connections in the land and way of seeing that might yet prove helpful. After all, if Christian Zionism has been part of the problem, contributing to the ideological rigidity in the land, then is it not the role of the church to deflate that ideology, and at least expose its

7. Karsh, *Palestine Betrayed.*

8. French historian Maxime Rodinson, whose books I used to read as an undergraduate in the Middle Eastern Library in Durham, puts it this way in *Israel and the Arabs,* 316: "The origin of the conflict lies in the settlement of a new population on a territory already occupied by a people unwilling to accept that settlement. This is as undeniable as it is obvious. The settlement may be justified in whole or in part; but it cannot be denied. Likewise, the refusal of the indigenous population to accept it may be thought justifiable, or it may not."

adherents to some of the darker, unspoken aspects of the history? I guess I would not be writing this book, if I didn't believe that. To that end, I find myself promoting these days a kind of alternative history, if only to expose the Christian community to stories that tend not to get a hearing, at least until recently, in the mainstream media. The story of Tom Hurndall is one such story.

Working for International Solidarity in Gaza, Tom Hurndall was shot and killed by an Israeli sniper on April 11, 2003, while trying to protect a Palestinian child who had strayed into the security zone. Without going into all the details, the IDF claimed that he was unsighted and posed a threat to the Israeli watchtower, whereas his father proved, incontrovertibly as well as successfully, that he was wearing an orange jacket and was most definitely identifiable as a noncombatant. The trial took place in Ashkelon, and the sentence of the Israeli soldier to eight years imprisonment was a remarkable moment in the history of the conflict. As far as Tom's parents were concerned, the obfuscation of the investigation, the constant delay tactics, and even the fact that the soldier convicted was a Bedouin, exposed a much deeper problem in Israel. In short, they believed the death of their son by Israeli fire, and the attempt to cover up, was symptomatic of a deep malaise in the national psyche. As a result of her two years going back and forth to Israel, Tom's mother saw enough of the brutality with which Palestinians are treated to write this letter to the British Prime Minister, Tony Blair:

> How loud do I have to shout and what language do I have to find to say that this is unacceptable in a civilised society? Mr Blair, I am asking you to challenge Mr Bush's support of his deeply immoral regime—which is cruel beyond human understanding and which I have seen for myself first-hand: the illegal demolition of houses, the destruction of olive groves, the process of depriving people of the possibility of earning a living, the closure of checkpoints, the cutting off of water and electricity, curfews, humiliation, terror . . . so it goes on. In short, the dehumanisation of people. Mr Bush's statement that "Israel has the right to defend itself" says it all and clearly demonstrates views that collude with

the perception of Israel as a victim. If ever there was
a level of aggression that far outstrips justification and
provocation, then here it is.[9]

Strong words indeed, from a British mother and, at the risk of
sounding cynical, possibly why the soldier in question was eventually brought to justice. Tom Hurndall was a British citizen, after all,
not a Palestinian refugee. His mother had means, albeit limited, to
pursue her case, whereas a Palestinian mother has none. But why
I think her evidence is compelling is because she gives firsthand
insight into what is commonplace among Palestinians living in
the occupied territories. Her experience of frustration, intimidation, and unbearable loss is an everyday occurrence among the
people she eventually came to meet because of the incident. Again,
it is not the only perspective to bring to bear on the Arab-Israeli
situation. That would be imbalanced and also dishonoring of so
many Jewish mothers who have lost sons and daughters. But what
revisionism is trying to secure is a much-needed hearing for a narrative that has remained largely hidden.

Jesus, the True Vine

Returning to my own journey, I realize now that I had plenty of
opportunity to consider this counter-narrative. Colin Chapman's
book *Whose Promised Land?*, which was published in 1983, was
a brave attempt to highlight some of the injustices. In the circles I
was moving in, however, Chapman's book was practically black-
listed. His attempts to wrestle with the question and present a
relatively unknown Palestinian angle were dismissed, typically,
as replacement heresy and not edifying for serious Bible believers. Having bought a copy of my own, I felt awkward reading it.

---

9. Hurndall, *Defy the Stars*, 231. See also Abuelaish, *I Shall Not Hate*, for a
compelling story of hope as well as reconciliation in the face of unconscionable
military aggression upon Palestinian civilians in the Gaza Strip. Holocaust
survivor Elie Wiesel commends the book as "a necessary lesson against hatred
and revenge."

I can remember, on one occasion, hiding it under a pile of other books, just in case.

Looking back on those times, I feel a bit like someone who was trapped in a cult. I hesitate to use that word, because I have dealt with many cults since in my work as a pastor, and Christian Zionism is most definitely not a cult. There is no organizational structure for a start, nor any real leadership. But why the word cult suggests itself to me now—maybe cultish is a better word—is because the vilification of people like Chapman, the dismissal of his work as politically dangerous (a charge which I imagine Gary Burge was subject to from the religious right in America), is the kind of rhetoric that cults engage in when they feel threatened. Did Chapman have a political angle? For sure. But that doesn't make him bogus. He was keen to introduce to the Christian public, in a manner which was constructive as well as fair, the grievances among Palestinians that produced an organization like the PLO. "However much we may want to condemn its activities as terrorism," he writes, "we must try to listen to what the movement is trying to do and say on behalf of the Palestinian people."[10] It's not good enough, he claims, to simply blame the Arab nations for not absorbing Palestinian refugees—an argument that is put forward by Christian Zionists time and again. Rather, it is incumbent upon all of us to wake up to the reality of so many "Naboth's vineyards,"[11] and try to discern what needs to be done. Politically dangerous is one way of describing this kind of rhetoric; prophetically challenging is another. And I imagine one of the reasons I became more willing to propound this kind of hermeneutic is because I started to realize that this is what my dissenting tradition had been doing for centuries: that is, speaking truth to power.

As I perceived it, the emergence of a growing body of revisionist critiques in the nineties, undoubtedly shaped by the war in Lebanon, as well as the Palestinian Intifada, coincided with a growing number of New Testament theologians offering a very different hermeneutic to that of Christian Zionism. Typically,

10. Chapman, *Whose Promised Land?*, 89.
11. Chapman, *Whose Promised Land?*, 173.

they were often branded as replacement theologians, and maybe in one or two instances the charge was justified. In reality, all they were trying to do was reflect the clear shift in thinking in the New Testament about the nature of the people of God, the law, the temple, and the land. It is not that they were antisemitic. If anything, New Testament theology post-Holocaust has been profoundly sympathetic to the confluence of Judaism and Christianity. What they were seeking to describe, however, is the radical inclusivity of the gospel of Jesus, the internationalism of the Christian church, and the relativization, therefore, of the land. Again, it would be disingenuous to say that there was no political agenda attached to this rather different hermeneutic. No theology is formed in isolation. But with one or two exceptions, it would be fair to say that these theologians were seriously trying to grapple with the biblical text and trying to explain why Christian Zionism represents, in their estimation, a naive and flat rendering of the grand narrative of the Bible.

For me, the best proponent of this thinking, at that time of reorientation, was the New Testament scholar Gary Burge. Again, there is no point denying that he had a political agenda. Practically half of his book *Whose Land? Whose Promise?* is an attempt to highlight what he regarded as human rights abuses on the part of the Israeli government.[12] But to say that his biblical hermeneutics is therefore just an extension of his politics is both to underestimate the caliber of his scholarship and conveniently avoid its contemporary application. One of the texts Burge cites as evidence of a shift in thinking on the question of land is John 15. The reason I took note of it all those years ago is because in the circles I was moving in John 15 was typically being used in a devotional fashion. "I am the vine, you are the branches," says Jesus. "If you remain in me, and I in you, you will bear much fruit."[13]

Burge doesn't disclaim this pietistic overlay of the text, but what he alerts us to, even so, is the political significance of the metaphors. After all, the vine is the chief biblical symbol of nationhood.

12. Burge, *Whose Land? Whose Promise?*
13. John 15:5.

Both the prophets and the Psalms utilize it to describe God's choice of Israel, the sacredness of the land, and her vocation to be a fruit-bearing people. That Israel has failed to do so is what turns Isaiah 5, the song of the vineyard, into an elegy, and Psalm 80 into a lament. Even so, despite the judgment, hope remains for a restored vine. Hence, when Jesus leads his disciples from the Upper Room, through the temple precincts, and points to the images of the vine that decorate the temple frescos, Burge is in no doubt as to the message our Lord means to convey. As with many aspects of Jewish faith in John's Gospel—the temple, the law, sabbath, the bread of heaven, resurrection—Jesus is now drawing the image of the vine to himself, not by way of replacement, but by way of fulfillment. With a subtlety that avoids gnosticizing on the one hand, and territorial literalism on the other, Jesus announces himself as the personification of the land and the climax of its promise.

As someone who subscribed to the Christian Zionist vision of a restored land, but had always struggled to reconcile this to the radical newness of the Jesus movement, this hermeneutical approach made a lot of sense. Without in any way detaching from the Jewishness of Jesus, or from the stock images of the Bible, the motif of fulfillment, which also occurs more explicitly in the Gospel of Matthew, deals with the fundamental problem many have with Christian Zionism which is the suggestion of a dual covenant. Christian Zionists deny this. They argue that the return to the land is a matter of covenant faithfulness, and can coexist alongside a transnational, multiethnic community, which is the church. But what this conviction fails to answer is the question of why a piece of land in the Middle East might be sacred when the whole earth is in fact the scope of our inheritance.[14] This is not to question the existence of the modern state of Israel. On the contrary. The return of Jewish people to the land is compelling, essential, and epic. Notwithstanding the solidarity we feel for Palestinian refugees, and our growing anxiety about right-wing nationalism, Christians have a moral duty to uphold and strengthen the state of Israel. To

14. Wright, *Climax of the Covenant*, 174.

frame this in messianic terms, however, is far more problematic than Christian Zionists are prepared to admit.

Christian Zionists cite their own biblical texts, of course, in support of their claims and spend a good deal of time in thorough exegesis. It is not as if they detach from the Bible. On the contrary. The appeal of Christian Zionism is that it claims biblical authority. Anything less would render it inconsequential. The question of whether Christian Zionism has biblical credibility, however, cannot simply be a matter of proof-texting, or even simple exegesis, but of critical acumen, otherwise all we have is a series of bible verses without any underlying theological method. I discovered this on the issue of women in leadership, which we explored as a church a few years ago. Line the texts up one way, and you get a conservative view; line them up another way, and you end up as an egalitarian. And so it is that the debate becomes a contest of texts rather than a serious theological discussion.

I note this problem as I read through Gerald McDermott's book *Israel Matters*.[15] By his own admission, McDermott began his spiritual journey as a supersessionist but then, through a series of conversations, repented of his position and became a Christian Zionist. In the opening chapters of the book, he tracks his thinking: he lists the various figures from church history who believed in the restoration of the Jews to the land, and then adumbrates a series of texts to support this view. He then presents, in the light of these commitments, a version of the present conflict, with relevant factual data, in which the Arabs come out as perpetrators and the Zionists as defenders.

As was noted earlier, the historiography around 1948 is largely determined by prior political commitments. McDermott is no exception: hence, no mention of the massacre of Deir Yassin, for example, but plenty of references to the failure of the Arab world to absorb Palestinian refugees. As much as I found that section irritating (the book was recommended to me by a friend who was concerned about my sympathies for Palestinians), it was his focus on single verses of Scripture, however, and beyond that

15. McDermott, *Israel Matters*.

his predilection for single words—their etymology, their meaning in the original language, the adequacy of the translation—that irritated me more. I guess we all do it. As preachers, we can find a word and so fixate on it that soon enough the word enlarges beyond all proportion to its place in the sentence. But in *Israel Matters* this becomes something of an art form.

For example, McDermott notes that the beatitude "Blessed are the meek, for they shall inherit the earth" (a translation that is so much part of our idiom of speech) should read "Blessed are the meek for they shall inherit *the land*."[16] He argues this on the basis of Psalm 37:11, which contains the Hebrew word *erets*, and which is a clear reference, he argues, to the land of Israel. From this McDermott makes the claim that "this beatitude was a sign that Jesus expected a future return of Jews to the land and a restored Jerusalem."[17] Quite apart from issues of transmission from the Masoretic text to the Septuagint, and then to the lexicon of the New Testament, the hermeneutical leap from the translation of one word to a statement about Jesus and a future return of the Jews is indeed a remarkable feat.

One could claim that Burge is guilty of the same thing when he argues, as I have just noted, for the incorporation of the notion of land in the image of Jesus as the vine. But why Burge's approach is credible, avoiding the kind of proof-texting that McDermott employs, is because the vine image coheres with the fulfillment motif throughout John's Gospel, thus allowing at least some tentative, if not conclusive, theological assertions about the symbolic world of Judaism in the light of Jesus, the Word made flesh. Even then, we can't be fully sure. For myself, Burge's textual work in John 15 simply opened a door. To move further away from Christian Zionism was more than a text for me (as I am sure that moving towards Christian Zionism was more than a text for McDermott) but a wholesale reimaging of the trajectory of Scripture for the sake of christology, pneumatology, and the mission of the church. It is in

---

16. McDermott, *Israel Matters*, 29–30.

17. McDermott, *Israel Matters*, 72.

this area that our debates ought to take place: not in word studies but in overarching biblical and theological themes.

It is worth noting that McDermott's conversion to Christian Zionism causes him to stress the continuities between Christianity and Judaism. He gets close to the view of E. P. Sanders, who famously argued that Paul's only issue with Judaism is that it was not Christianity. No surprise, therefore, that I trace my own journey away from Christian Zionism to a belief in the theological discontinuities between Christianity and Judaism. To assert these discontinuities alongside the continuities is not a dismissal of the fresh perspectives on Paul, of which Sanders is something of a founding figure, but simply what Christian orthodoxy requires. What kind of theology are we talking about that doesn't cohere with the startlingly new thing that occurs in the resurrection of Christ and the coming of the Spirit? To state the matter boldly, a theology that fails to properly celebrate the inauguration of the Kingdom of God in the events surrounding Jesus of Nazareth, failing also to realign ethics in the way that Jesus himself teaches— "You have heard it said . . . but I say to you"[18]—is not deserving of the description Christian. The death, resurrection, and ascension of Jesus, and the coming of the Spirit is *the* eschatological moment in Christian cosmology. The Christian community—which includes Jews as well as gentiles—is addressed to those upon whom the fulfillment of the ages has come.[19] To understate this, even in the interests of a Christian-Jewish rapprochement, is in fact a betrayal of the sheer genius of Christian revelation—what we might even refer to as its uniqueness.

My own development in the hard work of theological method began, strangely enough, at the other end of the spiritual spectrum. I spent the first decade of pastoral leadership addressing the highly contentious matter of prosperity theology, which didn't so much understate the eschatological moment of Christ and Spirit but, instead, was guilty of overstating it. To use Gordon

---

18. For the whole series of six antitheses, as they are often referred to, in the Sermon on the Mount, see Matt 5:21–48.

19. 1 Cor 10:11.

Fee's terminology, health and wealth teaching is an over-realized eschatology.[20] It is a very modern manifestation of what Luther might call "a theology of glory." Christian Zionism, on the other hand, is an under-realized theology. Its focus is end-times, to be sure. It exists for the sake of the Parousia. But the biblical trajectory by which it arrives at that place is a serious detraction, in my estimation, of the eschatological significance of the gospel. It is not that Christian Zionists cease to believe in salvation through Christ. They are Protestant evangelicals, whatever else they are. But by placing so much emphasis on the return of the Jews to the land, they have, by the same token, dulled what Tolkien might call the "eucatastrophe" of the gospel of Jesus Christ. As is the case with so much popular apocalyptic, the attempt to align dates and texts takes the faith into a cul-de-sac of speculative theology and away from the substantial core of Christian proclamation. In the process, it relegates prophetic utterance from the genre of imaginative speech to the game of predictive proof-texting.

My argument, thus far, is of course wide open to the charge of supersessionism. Having ministered at Millmead for two decades, I am acutely, if not painfully conscious of this accusation. I am also conscious that any attempt to shift the language away from words like replacement to that of fulfillment—Jesus is the fulfillment of the covenant story of God—is not only frowned upon as mere semantics, but also has the power to incite further anger, such are the sensitivities around this issue. But as a preacher of the gospel, which is primarily how my theology has formed over the years, what is one supposed to do? Handling the texts week after week, which is the routine privilege of any serious church pastor—and from where more theological reflection ought to emerge, in my opinion—leads you to only one conclusion: that the Christ event is so epochal, so utterly conclusive, as to render everything else subservient to its claim. Whether it is an Old Testament narrative or New Testament epistle, the compulsion of the Christian preacher is the new creation that is in Christ. This is not an excuse

20. For an extended discussion on over-realized eschatology, see Fee, *God's Empowering Presence*, 822–26.

for bowdlerizing the awkwardness of the life of King David, for example, or spiritualizing the enemies of the imprecatory Psalms. Too much of that occurs in Christian devotionals, turning every passage from the Old Testament into an altar call for Christ. What it does mean, however, is that all Christian theology, worthy of the name, must, of necessity, celebrate the radical newness of the incarnation. It must highlight not just the continuities of the story, which are manifold, but also the scandalous discontinuity with what has gone before. If that is replacement theology, then so be it. It seems that we have come to an impasse in the terms deployed on both sides of the debate. The point I am trying to make here, from my own vantage point as a pastor-scholar, is that what Christian Zionists call replacement is most times the honest attempts of Christian preachers to be faithful the gospel summons.

Christ at the Checkpoint

Returning to my own biography for a moment, by the time I arrived at Millmead, in the spring of 2004, I was already detached from Christian Zionism. As I have written about elsewhere, I was energized about the gospel, and was hoping that the assurances I had already given to the church about my love for the Jewish people, as well as the need to evangelize, would be enough to avoid too much controversy about my views concerning the land. But what I discovered, and why I never really bothered thereafter to articulate my position, is that nuance is not really an option for Christian Zionists. Such is their commitment to actual geography that even my love of the Jewish diaspora was regarded with suspicion. No matter that one might hold to an eschatology that includes the Jews. The fact that it didn't hinge on the restoration of the land rendered it inconsequential. It was frustrating to say the least.

The argument that was consistently put forward to me was the kind of argument you find in *Israel, God's Servant*, by David Torrance and George Taylor: namely, that if Israel's spiritual rejection of Jesus had a material dimension—meaning: the expulsion from the land—then by the same token her spiritual acceptance of Jesus, which is the promise held out in Romans 9–11, would involve a material restoration.[21] Anything less, according to the authors, is poor exegesis. But surely this is a case of profound eisegesis, a reading into the text? Even though it sounds logical, the reversal of exile by means of a return to the land fails to take into account, both in the text itself but also in the forward movement of the whole drama of Scripture, the radically new embodiment of God's promise in Christian communities made up of Jews and gentiles. According to N. T. Wright, the establishment of these ethnically heterogenous communities before the imminent destruction of the temple, explains the urgency of the Pauline mission.[22] For Christian Zionists to insist that God's purpose for the Jews reverts in the final instance to the land is not only literalistic, but anachronistic. It merges ethnicity with territory in a way that is both retrograde and unhelpful. Furthermore, to say that Jews around the world are coming to Jesus because of it, which is how Christian Zionists tend to envisage the grafting back into the people of God, is not only a strange way of justifying statehood, but also highly anecdotal. If anything, one could imagine that the impact of national identity on the Jewish diaspora would work in the opposite direction: not so much leading to Jesus but towards a revitalized Judaism. Jonathan Sacks says as much in *Future Tense*. Even without personal relocation to Israel, the mere presence of Jewish people in biblical terrain, he argues, is enough to excite the diaspora and unite it to the core.

Given the trajectory, as well as chronology, of my journey away from Christian Zionism, it will not surprise readers to know that the first decade of my tenure at Millmead, which I deemed a very fruitful time for the gospel, saw the departure of a whole number of people who came to realize that Israel was no longer going to be a central focus of the church. It's not that anyone was prevented from praying for Israel, but it wasn't going to be mainstream. What transpired, therefore, was a gradual exodus from Millmead to a nearby fellowship that truly was committed to Israel

21. Torrance and Taylor, *Israel, God's Servant*, 44–63.
22. Wright, *Paul*, 404–6.

and all things Jewish—including at times the lighting of sabbath candles. I must confess, I never really got that bit, even when I was a Christian Zionist. For a gentile Christian to commit to Jewish practices had always struck me as a bit odd. I had the same reaction to Christian choruses, if I am honest, that adopted Jewish rhythms. Quite apart from the fact we don't really know what ancient Jewish songs would have sounded like, the fact that we were singing them as if they were ancient was a bit awkward, to say the least. Nothing against tambourines, but to pretend we were reinventing Davidic praise was for me an issue of credibility.

It was around this time that I took my first trip into the West Bank. Thirty years on from my first trip to Israel, finally I got to see firsthand the disputed areas of what is referred to as Judea and Samaria, if you are a hard-line Jewish settler, or the occupied territories, as they are more commonly known. For obvious reasons, this mountainous central belt is not on the Israeli tourist map. Christian pilgrims who come to the Holy Land would hardly venture there, which is sad not least from a spiritual point of view. Some of the most venerated religious sites—for Jews, of course, as well as Christians—are in this part of the country. By not including them on the tour one is left with a truncated biblical narrative, but also a distorted political narrative. Bethlehem gives some exposure to the issues (and if you are fortunate enough to arrive there on January 6, which I did, inadvertently, you can witness firsthand the glorious chaos of an Orthodox Christmas). But it's nothing compared to visiting the West Bank, let alone Gaza, which I haven't yet visited. To view the Palestinian refugee camp of Balata, founded in 1950, on the outskirts of the city of Nablus, is to wonder at the sheer scale of the displacement from the *Nakba* to the present day. Densely populated with 300,000 residents, in an area of 0.25 square kilometers, it is a testament to the intractability of the political conflict, and the immense injustice that the Palestinians feel about their plight.

Viewed from the vantage point of Mount Gerizim, from where you can see the whole camp, it seems inconceivable that life could flourish in such a settlement. I had the same thoughts as I looked over the notorious France colony in Islamabad which, unlike Balata, I did stay in for a couple of nights in 2014. What made my impressions in Nablus more vivid was the juxtaposition of Balata to the some of the new Jewish settlements which we had so recently visited as we made our way east from Jerusalem. Not only are the Jewish settlements a provocation to the whole notion of a Palestinian state, they also highlight, by their sheer brilliance, the relative squalor of the Arab communities. For sure, the issues are complex. The territorial issues surrounding the West Bank, including matters of security, statehood, and peace, defy reasonable diplomacy. But this is not helped by the fervor of evangelical Christians whose ideology on this matter practically forecloses any reasonable debate. As far as Christian Zionists are concerned, the West Bank is not occupied territory. It didn't belong to anyone in the first place, so they argue. It is in fact the ancient biblical land of Judea and Samaria, recovered in 1967 as a result of the "hardening" of the Arab nations, and therefore, as befits the theology of hardening, regarded by Christian Zionists an act of sovereignty on the part of God.

Not only does this conviction appear in the literature of organizations like ICEJ; it also manifests in various phrases and gestures. I can recall, on more than one occasion, pro-Israel evangelicals pointing to the sky when the subject of the Six-Day War and the acquisition of the West Bank came up, as it often did in the eighties. No matter that the ensuing settlements consistently flout UN resolutions. As is always the case when ideology is at stake, opposition or criticism only serves to strengthen the righteousness of one's cause. In short, the more the world opposed the occupation, the more Christian Zionists felt strengthened in their support. As I imagine will happen with this book, criticism simply confirms the narrative.

In the political climate of the early eighties, the apocalyptic that Christian Zionists fostered was not particularly unique. This was the era of Menachem Begin and Ronald Reagan. Since then, things have become a bit more cynical. Certainly, Christian Zionism doesn't enjoy the same coverage that it received in those years. If anything, it suffers from a shift among evangelicals towards a more progressive theological vision. To put it bluntly, Christian Zionism doesn't fare very well in the woke agenda. But where it does receive encouragement is in the resurgence of the right-wing in Israel. As a matter of fact, my latest trip, forty years on from my first, coincided with an unannounced visit on the Temple Mount of the controversial Israeli National Security Minister, Ben Gvir. In the politics of Jerusalem, such a brazen act typically incites violence. This time it didn't. But that is not to say that tensions don't simmer, as everyone knows, just under the surface, thus making Israel a most volatile country.

Politically, the justification for settlements on the West Bank, and then of course the building of a wall, is that of security. For Christian Zionists, however, as indeed for ultra-nationalist Jews, the real issue is inheritance. Rather like the conquest under Joshua, which I have seen used in a church context as a motif for Bush's invasion of Iraq in 2003, the appropriation of God's gift of land to his chosen people is priority. It trumps everything. And such is the strength of conviction, there is no doubt in my mind that for most Christian Zionists the end justifies the means. The fact that the fulfillment of the prophetic vision may include a certain measure of "collateral damage" is simply unfortunate and not a reason to reassess.

It is perhaps this specific mindset, and the way it simply ignores the collective trauma that exists among ordinary Palestinians in these occupied territories, that contributed more than anything else to my growing unease with Christian Zionism in the late eighties. The first Intifada from 1987–1993, which I experienced firsthand in the summer of 1988 on a visit to Jerusalem, was not something that I could easily dismiss as rebelliousness. Rather, I began to register, and take seriously, the deep-seated frustrations that the Intifada represented, coming as it did twenty years on from the occupation. The closure of the shutters in the markets of the Old City of Jerusalem became for me a parable not of rebelliousness but of hopelessness. Conversely, the demonizing of the Palestinian

Intifada among certain strands of Christian Zionism became for me a cynical attempt to evade the issues.

In looking back at that time, it is difficult to recall whether my disaffection with Christian Zionism was a result of theological reassessment or political disillusionment. In other words, did a change in hermeneutics uncover what I was hitherto unable to see politically; or did my growing unease with right-wing politics in Israel, and its uncritical endorsement by Christian Zionists, cause me to seek an alternative way of interpreting Scripture? It is difficult to say. I suspect it was something like a symbiotic relationship. The one affected the other, until the position I was left with was practically a complete reversal of the one I started out with. These days I have managed to synthesize, and in part three I shall try to unpack what that might look like. But it is worth stating that to get to a synthesis, particularly on this subject, one has to first renounce what I now regard as a very peculiar theological agenda, including its inability to properly embrace the complexity of the present-day conflict. It is one thing to highlight the Balfour declaration. It was indeed a significant landmark in the history of the Jews. From a Palestinian perspective, however, its significance lies in what it doesn't say about the identity of the "non-Jewish" peoples who already live in the land. The same is true of the UN partition plan, which gave the majority Arab population less than half the land. To not even try to understand why it might have been unacceptable to the indigenous Palestinian communities is surely a case of selective memory. It is true that existential matters are at stake. The phrase "we will sweep them [the Jews] into the sea" is indeed haunting, and no fiction when it comes to groups like Hamas (see appendix 2). But to keep citing it as a way of evading the substantial grievances over partition, which is what tends to happen in evangelical portrayals of the conflict, not only begins to sound like a mantra, but also contributes to the unfortunate process by which history transforms into mythology. The Middle East is of course a battleground of mythologies—be it Zionist, Islamic, or even the mythologies of America and Russia. My suggestion is that Christian Zionism is perhaps the most potent mythology of all.

A painful irony in all of this, which was noted earlier, is the failure of evangelicals who are committed to the restoration of Israel to properly acknowledge the resident Christian community in the land, which is predominantly Arab. Caught between radical Islam on the one side, and right-wing settlers, on the other, being a Palestinian Christian in somewhere like Gaza, for example, or Nablus, or even Bethlehem, can be a challenging experience, to put it mildly. But this is further compounded by the almost complete indifference of Christian tourists to their plight. Indeed, the standard Christian tour of Israel, taking in Jerusalem and then Galilee, is itself an exercise in avoidance. In so far as these tours focus on biblical sites and fail to engage with the contemporary situation, they further exacerbate the frustrations of Arab Christians, and in some instances inflame anger by using the archaeology to legitimate Zionist claims to the occupied territories. It cannot be easy, for example, for Palestinians to see Christians drooling over the biblical archaeology of the biblical site of Shiloh which was excavated in 2006. As much as it is an important discovery and a venerated site, the fact that it is then used as evidence of Jewish presence in the land is not only rank politicization of archaeology (one supposes that all archaeology is political), but a further insult to the indigenous people.

For this reason, all Christian tours should include, in my opinion, a visit to the Tent of Nations, near Bethlehem. It may not be as comforting as a trip to the Church of the Nativity, and it certainly won't offer the souvenirs, but in terms of experiencing a rather different narrative, I regard it as compulsory. My own visit occurred in 2014, following an absence of just over two decades from Israel. Run by the Nasser family, on land they have owned the title deeds for as far back as Ottoman rule, Tent of Nations is a Christian community that has been repeatedly targeted by religious settlers from nearby Gush Etzion. Standing on the hilltop as dusk fell, one could see from the lights of the various settlements—Neve Daniel, Beitar Illit, Alon Shuvut, Elazar—how surrounded this community was, and how pressured it has felt to give up its land. Only a few weeks before our visit, some young Jewish men had turned up hoping through their intimidation to further erode the commitment of this community to stay. It achieved the very opposite, for here is a Christian community rooted in the very deepest traditions of nonviolence. At the entrance to the farm is a large stone on which are inscribed the words: "we refuse to be enemies." For the Nasser family this is not simply a text, an impressive slogan, but a guiding principle, and consistent with the surpassing righteousness that Jesus expects of his followers.[23] It occurs to me now, so many years later, that had this ethic been adopted by all sides in the conflict, the history of the region would be very different indeed. As naive as it sounds, I believe it may yet bring about change, as I hope to show in part three.[24]

We left the Tent of Nations that evening and traveled to Bethlehem to enjoy a meal with our host, a dear Palestinian Christian woman called Mary, following which we drove back to Jerusalem, first to drop Mary off at her home in East Jerusalem and then to return to our hostel in the Old City. If I was already moved by the story of the Nasser family, which has made the highest court in the land following an illegal eviction by the IDF, I was to be further affected as we crossed through the checkpoint late that night on our way out of Bethlehem. The queuing is one thing. This is a daily inconvenience for Palestinians traveling between different zones. But what was more disturbing was the treatment Mary received as she presented her papers to two young Israeli soldiers. Bearing in mind she was old enough to be their mother, had lived in Jerusalem all her life, and was clearly acting as our host, I would have thought a bit of courtesy was in order. Instead, she was questioned for over five minutes, leaving Mary not only feeling humiliated in front of her guests, but also deeply exasperated that this kind of treatment should be allowed. She didn't blame the soldiers as such. They were kids. She blames a psychology deeply embedded in Israeli society which makes a potential terrorist of every Palestinian (and, conversely, a fascist of every Israeli). The wall which

23. Matt 5:20; see also 5:47, where Jesus elucidates what a surpassing righteousness might mean in terms of love for one's enemies.

24. Braverman, *Fatal Embrace*, 3–6.

we drove alongside up to the checkpoint simply reinforces the pathology. Like every wall that has ever been built in the name of security, it is not the solution to the problem but an accentuation of the problem. Perhaps more painful in the end, for someone like Mary, is not the frustration of checkpoints, but the inaccessibility of holy sites. As journalist Janine de Giovanni notes,

> Since 1993, Palestinians living in the West Bank and Gaza have not been able to enter East Jerusalem without a permit, which is nearly impossible to obtain. This means Palestinian Christians are prevented from accessing some of the most sacred sites in Christianity. They cannot visit the wondrous and deeply moving Church of the Holy Sepulchre, built on the spot where Christ is said to have been crucified and buried . . . nor can Palestinians walk along the Via Dolorosa's Stations of the Cross . . . nor can they experience Gethsemane, a lush garden at the foot of the Mount of Olives, where, according to the New Testament, Jesus prayed in agony before Judas betrayed him.[25]

Mary didn't talk a great deal about this. By the time we dropped her off at her home in East Jerusalem, she was visibly exhausted. But I have since discovered that this is a very deep grief for the indigenous Christian Arab community. Naim Ateek, a Palestinian priest in the Anglican communion, puts it most poignantly in his book *Contemporary Way of the Cross*: "Our Via Dolorosa is not a mere ritualistic procession through the narrow streets of the old city of Jerusalem but the fate of being subjugated and humiliated in our own land."[26]

Two Coastal Cities

Before concluding this part of the book and moving on towards some kind of synthesis, I should like to describe a tale of two cities, which, although only twenty kilometers apart, may as well be on

25. de Giovanni, *Vanishing*, 74–75.
26. Quoted in Mayes, *Holy Land?*, 59.

different planets. I am talking about Ashkelon, where I once lived, and Gaza, which I have never been to. They share the same Mediterranean coastline, but in every other respect they diverge into two separate communities. During my two months in Ashkelon in 1983, which was in essence an orientation program to all things Israeli, I had no real knowledge, let alone contact, of the situation in Gaza. The plight of its people had yet to become the international news story that it is today. I hadn't realized, to my shame, that I was only a stone's throw from what would become one of the great humanitarian crises of our generation.[27]

As always, the politics is complex. I'm not about to simplify the situation into a contest of good versus evil. I may have qualms about the way some of the Israelis I met laughed at the ineptitude of the missiles sent by Hamas. The truth is, Israel's Iron Dome Air Defense system effectively neuters short-range missile attacks against towns like Ashkelon, and they gloated about that. Indeed, the way one woman described gathering on the beach with her neighbors, watching the missiles being plucked out of the sky, made it sound like a fireworks display. But then again, this is the same woman who every morning, as a young teacher during the seventies, would have to skirt the perimeter of her primary school, checking for bombs. So who am I to judge? I'm just a grammar school lad from Buckinghamshire.

Nevertheless, it is not a situation that has improved. If anything, the conditions in Gaza have worsened over the years. My own indication of this comes from trying to arrange a visit to one of the remaining Baptist churches in Gaza, via the Christian charity Open Doors, and being told, in no uncertain terms, that this would be an impossibility. As it was, I ended up traveling to Iraq with Open Doors in 2018. We were there to show solidarity with the beleaguered Christian community in Kurdistan—mainly Chaldean Orthodox churches—which had endured the unspeakable atrocities of Isis. I have also been in and out of Pakistan,

---

27. A reminder to the reader that I wrote this chapter in the summer of 2023, before the cataclysmic events of October 7 (and following) which took place in the vicinity of Gaza and Ashkelon.

both during martial law and in the aftermath of a suicide bomb on Easter Sunday at Gulshan Park, Lahore in 2016. But to enter Gaza, so I was told by my contacts, even under the auspices of Christian solidarity, was simply out of the question. The issue was not so much personal safety but political impenetrability. In short, I wouldn't be able to get a visa.

How it is that Gaza has become something of a prison for its inhabitants is a lengthy and troubled history. But how it is that the Israeli governments treatment of Gaza, specifically the disproportionate bombing of its civilians in retaliation for rocket attacks, has not been condemned by the Christian community is beyond understanding. To criticize Israel in this instance is not a case of antisemitism; rather, it is a case of moral integrity. As Bishop George Bell once argued, in his condemnation of the blanket bombing of German cities during the Second World War, the end doesn't justify the means. The use of unlimited power in reprisal is not the response of a civilized nation but is disturbingly close to the barbarism one seeks to counter.[28] For so many women and children to die in the demolition of terrorist hideouts is not an unfortunate case of collateral damage but of military reckless-ness. And to try to defend it, as some Christian fundamentalists attempt to do, on account of national security, and to complain at the same time about the way the media report these things, sim-ply confirms that Christian Zionism is an impenetrable ideology. Its reluctance to criticize gross militarism is not an expression of solidarity but surely a case of culpability. Perhaps more vividly than anywhere else in the Arab-Israeli conflict, Gaza reveals its intellectual paucity, and reminds me of Martin Luther King's warning about spiritual blindness. "Somewhere along the way," he argued, "the church must remind men that devoid of intelligence, goodness and conscientiousness will become brutal forces leading to shameful crucifixions."[29] That anyone could think that razing

---

28. For a discussion of the controversy around the blanket bombing of German cities in the Second World War, and Bell's condemnation of it in the House of Lords, see Chandler, *George Bell*, 112–21.

29. King, *Strength to Love*, 43.

Gaza to the ground, repeatedly and relentlessly, is justifiable on the grounds of national security, is an indication that brutality has already triumphed. Even though the conflict is framed by Christian Zionists as akin to David fighting Goliath—Israel against the world—in truth it is Goliath trouncing David. And in this modern narrative, Palestinian slingshots are simply no defense against military air strikes. The writer John Berger is insightful here, as well as indicting:

> The Israeli government claims that they are obliged to take these measures to combat terrorism. The claim is feint. The true aim of the stranglehold is to destroy the indigenous population's sense of temporal and spatial continuity so that they either leave or become indentured servants. And it's here that the dead help the living to resist. It's here that men and women make their decision to become martyrs. The stronghold inspires the terrorism it purports to be fighting.[30]

It is in this sense that Christian pastors/theologians like me struggle to understand the triumphalism among Christian Zionists about the possession of land, since land in the Old Testament was never simply a matter of acquisition, less so expansion, but of stewardship. Furthermore, there is a sense in which presence in the land was conditional on good stewardship. Contrary to the notion of land in perpetuity, which is integral to the Zionist ideology, the Scriptures present a rather more elusive notion of possession, as illustrated by the exile, in which land is gifted on the basis of fidelity to the grand themes of justice, mercy and humility. In the absence of these things, there is no land—or none that has any spiritual import. Instead, we find prophetic indictment, of a depth that is truly astonishing and is, arguably, the real genius of what it is to be Israel.

Certainly, that is how I began to see things in the late eighties. As a Christian theologian, a pastor, and preacher to boot, it simply made sense to read the first testament through this radical hermeneutic, not least because it cohered so beautifully with the

30. Berger, *Hold Everything Dear*, 64.

message of Jesus. Through the fresh perspectives of New Testament theologians like N. T. Wright and Marcus Borg, I came to see that Jesus himself was reworking this prophetic tradition, summoning his own generation to abandon what Borg terms "the politics of holiness" and instead recover the true center of its faith which is "the politics of compassion." Why else did Jesus encounter such opposition? Why else was he compared to Jeremiah, and alluded so often to his message? Because like Jeremiah, he dared to critique the temple, and challenged its so-called inviolability with the more fundamental issue of whether Israel was being true to her ethics. At which point, it became all too clear to me that God's word in the Middle East was nothing to do with territorial expansion, less so the reconstruction of a temple, but with the rather more awkward question of what to do with the foreigner in the midst. As Jeremiah makes clear in his blistering "the temple of the Lord, the temple of the Lord" sermon,[31] and as Jesus will replicate in his own indictment of temple ideology, the Lord is no respecter of sacred spaces. More important than the mechanics of worship is the matter of mercy.

Again, none of this means to deny the right of modern-day Israel to exist. Nor is it to demythologize the land. Myths are important to all of us, and the fact that many Jews have returned to their ancestral home, to a topography that one can read about in the Bible, is, by any standard, a remarkable history. As confusing as this might sound, I am even willing to respect that many regard this as prophetic fulfillment. What any civilized and intelligent person cannot accept, however, be they Christian, Jew, Muslim or otherwise, is election without responsibility. To put it crudely, if you think you are a chosen people, then you ought to act like that.[32] And unless we simply resort to a trajectory of conquest, which is the agenda of the far right in Israel, then the inconvenient

31. Jer 7:1–15.

32. In this regard, I have never quite understood the veneration by Christian Zionists of the British Military Officer Orde Wingate. His passion for the Bible is legendary, but so also is his military aggression against the Arabs, not to mention incidents of sadism. For a fuller treatment of this rather eccentric military figure, see appendix 1.

political reality, as far back as the Balfour declaration, is that there is another people group, with their own narrative history, who share the same territory. To criminalize that history is not simply brutish, but unimaginative.[33]

The same applies to all nations. Exceptionalism doesn't mean exemption from the normal rules of engagement. Nor does it permit recklessness, however righteous you believe your cause to be. Rather, it demands higher standards. It requires you to live out the ideals you have set yourself. That this might incur a greater stringency—from the media, for example—that is not required of others may appear like double standards, and in some instances it is. But it may also be the kind of rigor we might expect to see when dealing with a country that claims, among other things, to be the only effective liberal democracy in the Middle East. Protests on the streets of Israel in the early part of 2023 against the perceived dictatorial and ideological trends of the Netanyahu government is evidence that some of this critique is still capable of taking place internally. In the absence of a strong peace movement, or an effective left wing, this is a healthy sign. It doesn't detract from issues of security, but it rightly signals a fear of tyranny.

Divine Violence

As I write these sections, I am conscious there is a theological elephant in the room which any proper treatment of Christian Zionism must address: the matter of the conquest under Joshua. Apart from a few extremist voices, I don't recall anyone using it to legitimate inheritance rights. Typically, that is assigned to the patriarchal narratives. Even so, the destruction of Canaanite cities, involving the killing of women and children, is so integral to the trajectory of the story of Israel that neither can it be overlooked. It does in fact demand to be addressed, particularly by Christians whose teachings charter a very different course of

---

33. See Katanacho, *Land of Christ.* Katanacho offers a Palestinian perspective on the story of Hagar, seeing her plight as parabolic of his own people, but also a sign of hope.

nonviolence. In such a theological matrix, how might violence of such devastating consequences, not to mention the imprecations in the Psalter, be understood?

To address this problem thoroughly would take us beyond the parameters of this book. This can only be an excursus. But it is an important excursus, nevertheless, because the presentation of such violence in the canon of Scripture, not as a criminal injustice but as a legitimatized command, cannot be easily tidied away. However much we try to ignore it, conquest presses upon our moral conscience, and given the sheer topography of the land, let alone the theology, is uncomfortably relevant to the contemporary issue we are looking at.

Perhaps the most innovative treatment of the subject, and one that possibly reconciles the two testaments, is the work of Walter Brueggemann, who sees in the conquest not the assertiveness of a colonial power but the dismantling of empire.[34] To achieve this approach Brueggemann posits a difference between the actual words spoken to Joshua, which is restricted to burning the chariots and hamstringing the horses, and the words that come from the tradition, passed down from Moses, which become the rationale for cleansing the land of its inhabitants. Even if this doesn't fully circumvent the problem, it does at least suggest a way of reconciling the conquest narratives with the gospel imperatives. As Brueggemann so typically argues, the Old Testament must be read as advocacy of a very different witness to God's actions in the world. Taking Exodus as the pivotal moment, freedom from oppression is the key motif of the conquest, but also the key criteria by which Israel will be judged. Hence, the prophetic denunciation of monarchy where Israel becomes like any other nation in the stockpiling of wealth and weaponry. As Brueggemann asserts: "if Israel imitates the foreign kingdoms or is seduced by their power or their gods, Israel will also become an agent of domination."[35]

The contemporary relevance of Brueggemann's theology is never too far from the surface (Bush's invasion of Iraq often appears

---

34. Brueggemann, *Divine Presence amid Violence.*

35. Brueggemann, *Divine Presence amid Violence,* 53.

in his reflections), and ought to be apparent here in the matter of Christian Zionism: that the use of the conquest narratives to legitimize occupation or invasion or, worse still, ethnic cleansing is a serious category mistake. For all their apparent violence, they are in fact highly stylized narratives which have at their fore not an endorsement of power but a dismantling of power and, furthermore, a vision of a just and equitable society. This is not reading into the texts, nor political anachronism, but germane to the whole drama of Scripture, climaxing in the person of Jesus, who himself subverts messianic and military glory with cruciform love.[36] Anything less than this, no matter how seductive the ideology, betrays not just the universality of the gospel invitation but the radical generosity of the whole of Scripture. The reason God's injunction to Joshua is modest and restrained, dealing only with chariots and horses, is because Israel, from its very conception, is to live "not by might, nor by power, but by my Spirit."[37] "Prophetic faith," by which Brueggemann means our faith, "sets the inscrutable power of Yahweh over against the pretensions of state power. This paradigmatic antithesis is acted out already in the Exodus narrative."[38]

How strange then, as well as ironic, that Christian Zionism works a very different trajectory that, while not entirely uncritical of Israel, seems to have no trouble endorsing the military might of America in support of Israel.[39] In terms of mythmaking, the narrative presented is that of Israel's imminent annihilation. As noted earlier, the Six-Day War continues to be framed in these terms.

---

36. I had the privilege of writing an endorsement for the new Paternoster edition of Brueggemann's book. My editor, Robin Parry, wanted a quote from the church as well as the academy, and I was honored to offer it: "With typical panache Brueggemann goes a long way in helping us to reconcile the violence against God's enemies in the Old Testament with the love of the marginalized in the New. In the present climate of violence, *Divine Presence amid Violence* is a must-read."

37. Zech 4:6.

38. Brueggemann, *Divine Presence amid Violence*, 58.

39. For a sharp critique of American exceptionalism, and a positive understanding of the ethnic heterogeneity of the church, see Boyd, *Myth of a Christian Nation*.

But as Palestinian historian Rashid Khalidi argues, Washington knew otherwise. Government documents published since the war confirm that "Israel's military in 1967 was far superior to the militaries of all the Arab states combined, as it was in every other contest between them."[40] Which is not to say that Israel doesn't face issues of national security. That would be preposterous. But it is to say that it is disingenuous to enact crude and oftentimes reckless militarism under the pretext of existential threat. We are quick to identify this in the case of Russia; we ought to be able to identify it in the case of Israel, however uncomfortable it makes us feel. Furthermore, if we are to make a truly Christian contribution to the global scene, we would do well to place the conquest motif in the context of the whole of Scripture and, rather like Brueggemann, appropriate the prophetic radicality that lies at the very heart of the narrative. To be Israel is not to take matters into her own hands. That way lies disaster, as Isaiah was quick to point out to King Ahaz.[41] Rather, to be Israel is to eschew the way of the world and place one's trust in God.

A Cursed Victory

In setting out to chronicle my disquiet about the theology of Christian Zionism, my aim is not to convert its followers away from it. Given the strength of feelings, that would be a most unlikely outcome, and not one I want to burden myself with. To write with such a purpose would not only turn my prose into polemic but would also end up as a battle of biblical proof-texts, rather than a considered reflection, both historical and theological, on the complexities of the situation. I hope I am offering something in that order.

---

40. Khalidi, *Hundred Years' War on Palestine*, 96–97.

41. Isa 7:1–9. The theme of spiritual quietism in Isaiah—"in quietness and trust is your strength," Isa 30:15—is not an example of soft devotionalism, but political challenge: the imperative to trust God for one's battles, rather than rely on worldly alliances.

To restate my thesis again: Israel has a right to exist. Even if one does not share in the prophetic ideology of Zionism, the return of Jews to Palestine is legitimate and defensible. What is not defensible, and ought to trouble the Christian conscience more than it does, is the expansion of Israeli territory into occupied land, with all the social and economic ramifications this involves. In any other context, this would be the stuff of Christian charity. The plight of the Palestinians would, in normal circumstances, arouse numerous appeals. But because it is Israel, for some reason different rules apply. The ideological freight that the land has had to bear, for over a century now, seems to prevent perspicacity. For example, Christian Zionists argue that the territories gained after 1967 were always disputed territories, and therefore not occupied territories. In other words, there is no green line. But this is not true. This is simply a case of distorting history to suit ideology. Others, however, including a growing number of Israeli voices, are beginning to challenge this narrative. With a courage that ought to disturb Christian Zionists, they are preaching that occupation strikes at the very heart of what it means to be Israel. To use the language of Ahron Bregman, occupation turns the euphoria of the Six-Day War, which for him included his first visit as a little boy to Jerusalem, into a "cursed victory."[42] In reality, it is not an occupation, nor even an enlightened occupation, but an annexation.

Bregman is interesting because he is an Israeli who, as a result of doing his military service in Gaza, and then living through the Intifada, left the country in 1988, vowing never to return until the occupation was ended. To this day he lives in exile in the UK. Because of his stance, as well as his writing, he is tagged by his detractors as unpatriotic—an opprobrium often used of people who speak out. I regard him, however, as unmistakably patriotic. Like Jeremiah, who himself was accused of treason for speaking out, it was precisely for love of country that Bregman protested, because he couldn't equate what was happening in the occupied territories with the ideals of what it meant to be a citizen of his beloved Israel. To use George Orwell's distinction, he was patriotic

42. See Bregman, *Cursed Victory.*

at the very point at which he refused to be nationalistic. It is a courageous position to adopt. It places him in the company of people like Thomas Merton and Dietrich Bonhoeffer, whose moral vision compelled them to counter the militarism of their governments with an internationalism, or maybe a better word is ecumenism, that embraces all peoples of the world.[43]

Interestingly, as is increasingly the case among political commentators, Bregman sees no other option than a two-state solution. Hence, what bothers him about occupation, and the unremitting advance of Jewish settlements in the West Bank, is not only the increasing unlikelihood of a Palestinian state, but the growing likelihood, therefore, of Israel becoming an apartheid state. As shocking as it sounds, there is a logic to this. In order to maintain itself as a democracy in which Jewish identity is predominant, then the only way to safeguard it from a growing Arab demographic is to revert to discrimination as well as segregation. In one sense this is already happening. Technically, the status of Israeli Arabs is the same as any other citizen. Furthermore, there is data to suggest a positive view of the Israeli state among the Arab minority. In reality, however, many claim to being treated as second-class citizens—a perception that will only increase, Bregman warns, if the political situation remains unresolved.

---

43. For a celebration of radicals like Merton and Bonhoeffer, see Inchausti, *Subversive Orthodoxy*.

Part Three

Towards an Evangelical
Theology of Israel

Crossing the Line

IT IS OVER FORTY years ago now since I touched down at Ben Gurion airport and made my first visit to Israel. It is strange recall-
ing the memories of that time. And strange to reread some of the
Christian Zionist literature that so gripped me as a new convert
to Christian faith. I tend not to read fundamentalist theology
these days, so it was a bit of a shock. The rhetoric is strident. And
although some of the organizations these days are a little more
nuanced, nevertheless the ideology remains unchanged, including the antipathy towards replacement theology, which includes
anything that falls short of full-blown Zionism.

As I look back at that time, I feel a bit awkward, if I am honest, that I subscribed so passionately to such a theology. I don't
mean to be snobby. Like Richard Mouw, I do think there is a place
for the drama of fundamentalism. I may have a PhD, but I am still
given to making altar calls from time to time. Why not? At some
point, we all have to cross the line.[1] My problem with Christian Zi-

1. Mouw, *Smell of Sawdust*.

onism, however, is that it draws a line in the wrong place, making our faith contingent on whether we support Israel or not. The following paragraph, taken from a pamphlet, which I found in the archives at Millmead, is typical of the genre of that time:

> Now, because of our scarred history since 1917, when we have done far more to obstruct than to assist in Israel's Restoration, The Lord is now very angry with Britain (Zechariah 1:15). "We have not listened to your servants the prophets, who spoke in Your name to our kings, our princes, and our fathers, and to all the people of the Land . . . O Lord, we and our kings, our princes and our fathers are covered with shame because we have sinned against You" (Daniel 9:6, 8).

What is notable about this piece of rhetoric is that the calumny is attributable not just to individuals but to nations—in this instance Britain. As is clearly stated, the failure to actively pray for Israel and contribute to the restoration in the land, which many Christian Zionists here believe the British government has been guilty of, carries a penalty of spiritual decline. In short, if Britain's support for the restoration of Israel, through historical figures such as John Owen, John Wesley, Lord Shaftesbury, Robert Murray McCheyne, and Bishop J. C. Ryle, contributed to Britain's ascendency in the world, so her apparent betrayal of Israel since the Balfour Declaration in 1917 has contributed to her demise—or so the logic runs.

Looking back now at the literature, and the highly idiosyncratic approach that Christian Zionism takes on matters of biblical hermeneutics, it is difficult to believe how a History and Politics undergraduate from Durham University, with access to the superb Middle East Library just across Prebends bridge, could believe such things. Empires, by definition, rise as fall, as Paul Kennedy convincingly argues. The seeds of their demise can be discerned in the financial costs of sustaining them—the British empire being no exception.[2] To believe otherwise, or more specifically to believe that Britain lost her empire over the supposed failure to honor the

---

2. Kennedy, *Rise and Fall of the Great Powers*.

Balfour declaration, is just plain silly. Quite apart from the moral questions that attach to the notion of empire, not to mention the oddity of a twentieth-century nation being drawn into an Old Testament curse formula, the idea that Britain's loss of power relates to her abstaining on the UN vote for partition—which is one of the charges made—is as preposterous as the thesis put forward by Elie Halevy that Britain avoided a French Revolution because of the rise of Methodism.[3] No wonder people think fundamentalism is unintelligent. It's one thing to preach the foolishness of the cross. Christ crucified does indeed subvert reason and is a stumbling block. Likewise, certain aspects of Christian eschatology do appear incredulous but for faith. That much is true, and not something to be ashamed of. But to add to that a view of history that is speculative, which introduces extrabiblical events and gives them the status of gospel, is presumptuous, to say the least.[4]

As is so often the case with religious fundamentalists, the invective deployed against anyone who doesn't share their conviction is forceful. For Derek Prince, the attitude of Britain towards Israel and our subsequent moral decline requires nothing less than national repentance. Again, quite apart from the fact that this presupposes a view of British nationhood that is borderline imperial, the effect of this language means there is little room for debate. You either repent or you perish. In my early twenties, with minimal theological acumen, this was persuasive—impressive even. To think one could affect Britain's global status by repenting over Israel was thrilling. These days I see it as erroneous. It is akin with the thought world of British Israelites. As with some of the right-wing

---

3. As my old professor Reg Ward noted regarding the Methodist revival, in many ways it was a disrupter of social order not a pacifier. For an authoritative account of the Great Awakening, see Ward, *Protestant Evangelical Awakening*.

4. One notes this in the work of Murray Dixon, former rector of Christ Church, Jerusalem. In an otherwise informative book, Dixon makes all the quasi-utopian connections between the flourishing of the land and the return of the Jews to the land. He even cites research that David Pawson undertook about rainfall in Israel which led him to conclude that "periods when larger numbers of Jewish people made aliyah were marked by greater rainfall and that this was specially pronounced in 1948, the year Israel was reborn." Dixon, *Israel*, 200.

views for Brexit, such doctrines, which teachers like Derek Prince propound, accords Britain a special covenant status with God and, more importantly, has the effect of displacing the focus away from the dogmatic core of the gospel and onto territorial claims.

It occurs to me now, having had a chance to reflect more deeply on the matter, that Christian Zionism is not only a challenge for evangelicals like me, but also problematic for the very people it is trying to support: namely, the Jews. As my friend Melissa Raphael pointed out to me, because Christian Zionists are so eager to hasten the end-time apocalyptic and usher the return of Christ to Jerusalem, what happens is that they, inadvertently perhaps, end up instrumentalizing the Jews for their own purpose.[5] When I have raised this in conversation with Christian Zionists, it is often met with a certain measure of disdain. To instrumentalize a people for one's own agenda is a serious charge. But when you examine further, instrumentalizing is precisely what Christian Zionists are doing. By their own criteria, without the restoration of the Jews to the land, Jesus simply cannot return—the critical text being Acts 1:11, where the angel says to the disciples, who had just witnessed the ascension of Jesus on the Mount of Olives: "This same Jesus, who has been taken from you into heaven, will come back in the same way you have seen him go into heaven."[6]

Quite apart from the cosmological issues around the ascension of Jesus, the necessity of the restoration of Israel—Jerusalem more specifically—as a prerequisite for the Parousia surely begs further enquiry since, in almost every respect, the New Testament relativizes the centrality of the city in the purposes of God. Indeed, there are occasions when it appears completely obsolete. St. Paul's derogation of the present Jerusalem over against the freedom of the Jerusalem that is above—Gal 4:25–26—is not an

---

5. A view shared by Israeli historian Shlomo Sand, who also notes, more sinisterly, that despite their admiration for the Jews, the "overarching conceptions" of early Christian Zionists "regarding the members of this group did not differ fundamentally from the attitudes of Judeophobes." Sand, *Invention of the Land of Israel*, 172.

6. Acts 1:11.

antisemitic slur but the inevitable conclusion of a theology that begins with Jesus himself.[7]

A Fallen City

As someone who loves the city of Jerusalem, who was enchanted on that very first visit as I walked through the Damascus Gate, its obsolescence is a hard thing even for me to embrace. An eschatological vision that doesn't include this most historic location does seem strange, I admit, and dangerously close to a spiritualizing of the whole story of salvation. What is under consideration here, however, is not the spiritual over against the physical, but rather the universal over against the national. In other words, does the story end back in Jerusalem or does it go forth from Jerusalem to the ends of the earth?

In his comprehensive survey *Jesus and the Holy City*, Peter Walker demonstrates that the movement is unmistakably centrifugal. For all the lingering connectedness to Jerusalem after the resurrection, it is not long before the gospel is moving outwards from Judea, to Samaria, to the ends of the earth. Notwithstanding Paul's collection among his churches for the poor back in Jerusalem, the main impetus of his ministry is in the other direction: the desire to reach Spain with the gospel of grace; and also, as N. T. Wright points out, the urgency of forming heterogenous churches across the Mediterranean—Jewish and gentile believers together as one people—before the destruction of Jerusalem when of course everything would become so much more problematic. As Walker states at the end of his summary of Paul's view

7. I am mindful that so much of New Testament exegesis can be deeply hurtful to Jews. Commenting on Paul's scandalous recasting of the biblical narrative to make the matriarch Sarah the mother of Christianity, and Hagar the representative of Judaism, which effectively is what he does in Gal 4:21–31; and then of course Paul's argument here in Rom 9:10–13 that biological descent from Abraham is not enough to make you a child of the promise, Jonathan Sacks quite reasonably remarks how hard it must be "for a Christian to understand how a Jew feels when he or she reads these texts. It feels like being disinherited, violated, robbed of an identity." Sacks, *Not in God's Name*, 96.

of the Holy City—and with an eye to F. F. Bruce's classic statement that Jerusalem was to be the "place from which the crowning phase of the salvation of mankind would be displayed."[8]—"The physical city of Jerusalem, for all its previous significance, could no longer serve as the centre of God's people. There was a now a new centre—not Jerusalem, but Jesus."[9]

The idea of Jerusalem as a fallen city, no longer integral to the purposes of God, is a haunting one. It relegates what was once the glorious city of God to something like a ruin. But in the pre-Constantinian church this is effectively how Jerusalem was perceived. It's not that veneration disappeared altogether. Simon Sebag Montefiore in his magisterial book *Jerusalem: The Biography*, notes that Jewish Christians, led by Simon, son of Cleopas, returned to Jerusalem after the destruction, and started to honor the Upper Room.[10] Furthermore, there is evidence that Christians visited the sites of the crucifixion and the resurrection in Aelia Capitolina, as Jerusalem was known, beneath Hadrian's temple to Jupiter. But these are exceptions. With the arrival of Helena, however, mother of the Christian emperor Constantine (AD 248–328), Jerusalem revived in the consciousness of Christian historiography, although even here it was not on account of any eschatological vision but rather on account of its historical importance. So much of what we experience today by way of Christian pilgrimage, including the church of the Holy Sepulchre, goes back to Helena's own pilgrimage to Jerusalem, thus giving surprising authenticity to so many of the tourist sites, but also confirmation that the significance of Jerusalem for the Christians, here on in, would be spiritual veneration, not apocalyptic revelation.[11] This is what gives Jerusalem its character and why so many Christians visit the Holy Land today. It has practically nothing to do with prophetic promise. Christian Zionism in that sense is a Protestant aberration. Rather, a visit to

---

8. Bruce, "Paul and Jerusalem," 25.

9. Walker, *Jesus and the Holy City*, 160.

10. Montefiore, *Jerusalem*, 159.

11. For a fascinating survey of the importance of place in Judea and Galilee, see Ryan, *From the Passion to the Church of the Holy Sepulchre*.

the Holy Land acts like a devotional, allowing the pilgrim to visit the sites. It is the wonder of the incarnation not the promise of restoration that motivates, certainly as far as the Catholics and the Orthodox are concerned. Indeed, in the nineteenth century Jerusalem practically existed for the Orthodox pilgrims traveling all the way from Odessa on the Black Sea to visit the holy places.

A Holy Land

Vestiges of that golden era can be found right across the city: the church of Mary Magdalene near the garden of Gethsemane, with its gilded onion domes; the lesser-known church of the Holy Trinity in the Russian compound; Sergei's Courtyard, also in the Russian compound, which gave lodging to rich pilgrims, royalty and dignitaries; and the almost unidentifiable Alexander Nevsky church, near the church of the Holy Sepulchre. This last site looks more like a hostel than a holy place but, along with the other buildings, is evidence of a remarkable Russian presence which, under President Putin, is seeking to reassert itself in the Holy Land. Indeed, the poignancy of my visit to the Alexander Nevsky church in the January of 2023 was that of being greeted at the door by a young Ukrainian nun. I was not about to engage her in a conversation about the Russian invasion of her country a year earlier. But it did strike me as interesting, speaking as a historian, that Jerusalem continues to reflect, if not spark, the tensions that exist in European politics. What with the minor skirmishes I witnessed in Bethlehem on Orthodox Christmas Day, happening at the time of a major European war, it was in a very small way possible to imagine how clashes in the church of the Holy Sepulchre in the mid-nineteenth century ended up on the battlefields of the Crimea. Orlando Figes calls it the last truly religious war in Europe, but Putin's quasi-religious crusade, which includes a very strong Jerusalem component, makes this assessment a bit premature, in my opinion.[12] Retracing the Russian presence in the holy

12. See Figes, *Crimea.*

city didn't feel just historical; at the risk of sounding apocalyptic myself, it felt very contemporary. Russian imperialism is alive and kicking in twenty-first-century geopolitics. But again, the allure of Jerusalem for the Orthodox (by which I mean the devout) is not the evangelical dream of Jewish restoration but the much more devotional longing for connectedness to the gospels. Significantly, in the little shop at the church of Mary Magdalene, right next to the wayside shrine to the Romanovs, there were numerous pilgrim guides, in Russian of course, offering brief reflections on the various Christian sites around Jerusalem.

As with so many religious centers, entering through the gates that Thursday morning (the church is only open to the public two mornings a week) into the tranquillity of the gardens and then up to the church itself, felt like a journey into a lost world, a step back into a different century. The relics of Princess Ella, murdered by the Bolsheviks in Moscow during the White terror, certainly gave the church an added mystery. And they underline the fact that, despite its displacement as the epicenter of faith, Jerusalem retains an important place in the spiritual sensibilities of the worldwide Christian community. Whether it is Russian Orthodox, Greek Orthodox, Syrian Orthodox, Roman Catholic, Mar Thoma, Armenian, Lutheran, Anglican, Baptist, Pentecostal, or any other denomination, having a stake in Jerusalem, and in the Holy Land, helps to avoid the insidious pull towards Gnosticism. By visiting Jerusalem, and by touring places like Galilee, we rehearse once more what the theologians call the scandal of particularity; we recover the importance of place; we remember that there is nothing abstract about the faith. Names matter. The notice that reads "Jesus of Nazareth, King of the Jews" was meant as mockery; what it actually does is underline the spirituality of geography. Gnosticism is contemptuous of place. It takes the drama of the gospel and turns it into pithy sayings, abstract ideas. The gospel, on the other hand "is emphatically geographical. Place names—Sinai, Hebron, Machpelah, Shiloh, Nazareth, Jezreel, Samaria, Bethlehem, Jerusalem, Bethsaida—these are embedded in the gospel.

All theology is rooted in geography."[13] And can there be a more fascinating geography than that which corresponds with the lands of the Bible? It's not just the tourist sites that fascinate (which are more authentic than you think); nor just the obvious places, like Bethlehem. It is just the sheer topography: the contours of the land, the transition between the coastal plain and the Judean desert; the steep gradient from Jerusalem down to the Dead Sea; the contrast between Galilee in the north and the Negev in the south; the fact that you can sit at Jacob's well, which really is as deep as the Samaritan women said, and one side is Mount Gerizim and on the other side Mount Ebal.

It is a cliche, I know, but by visiting Israel the Bible comes alive. By traveling around the country, which for me includes further trips into countries like Lebanon, Egypt, Turkey and Jordan, you can so immerse yourself in the land that Scripture takes on a whole new depth. For a preacher, this is invaluable. I try to encourage young ordinands to get out to the Holy Land as quick as they can. "Don't leave it to your retirement," I say, "but get out there at the beginning of your ministry." It makes a difference. By traveling as a pilgrim rather than a tourist, one returns not with a bunch of cheap sermon illustrations but rather with a way of looking at Scripture that is earthy as well as prayerful. And by tracking the gospels on one of these trips, it simply reinforces why Christian Zionism is such an oddity. Landscape, text and memory combine on pilgrimage to accentuate both the particularity of the gospel and the universality of its scope. To put it in pilgrim language, walking in the footsteps of Jesus is to walk beyond nationalist symbols into a new world where partisanship gives way to people.

A good illustration of this is the story of Jesus and the woman at the well in John 4. Because of its location in Nablus, it tends not to feature on a classic tour of the Holy Land, which is a shame because of all the gospel sites it is one of the most vivid. Jacob's well, which these days is located within an Eastern Orthodox Church, is indeed deep—135 feet apparently. It takes a good twenty seconds or so for coin to plink in the water. Just above the church, or the well I

13. Peterson, *Under the Unpredictable Plant*, 129–30.

should say, is the mountain where Samaritans worship, as Jesus so respectfully acknowledged, remembering that only 70 kilometers south is Jerusalem, where "we Jews" worship.[14]

It wasn't until I embarked one summer on a short preaching series on Jesus and the Samaritans that I registered the significance of that part of the dialogue. The antipathy of Jews towards Samaritans was something I was conversant with. It is what makes the parable of the Good Samaritan in Luke 10 so shocking.[15] What I hadn't appreciated was the antipathy of Samaritans towards the Jews. As Gerard Russell points out in *Heirs to Forgotten Kingdoms*, such is the disdain Samaritans feel to this day about the temple in Jerusalem that they refuse to use the name David of any newborn boy.[16] As far as Samaritans are concerned, Mount Zion and the Davidic project is an aberration from the true narrative which is centered on the Pentateuch and the temple on Mount Gerizim.

All the more remarkable, then, that Jesus should engage in conversation with her, and all the more astonishing that Jesus relativizes both Jerusalem and Gerizim in his pursuit of worship that is "in Spirit and in truth." Again, this is not to say that Jesus is detached from his moorings, less so that he might be a Samaritan. Salvation is indeed from the Jews, asserts the Gospel of John, despite the reputation it has for being antisemitic. But with the coming of the Messiah, worship transcends these tribal differences and moves forward to a cultus that is no less embodied but universal, nevertheless, in its horizon. As Timothy Radcliffe notes in conversation with Łukasz Popko concerning the flow of the dialogue between Jesus and the woman: "The more personal it gets, the more it touches other people. The Word became flesh in a very particular

---

14. The well itself is of course a venerated site, given by the patriarch Jacob, who drank from it himself as did his sons and livestock.

15. See Borg, *Jesus*, 159, who argues convincingly that the parable of the good Samaritan in Luke 10:29–37 is in fact a scathing critique of "the politics of holiness" in which matters of ritual cleanliness have become more important than the fundamental vocation of Israel to show mercy—what Borg terms "the politics of compassion." The fact that it is a Samaritan who enacts mercy on the road between Jerusalem and Jericho is the sting in the tail of the parable.

16. Russell, *Heirs to Forgotten Kingdoms*, 176.

man, with his very personal story which becomes universal, the story in which we can all find ourselves."[17]

Since we are considering Jesus's interaction with a foreign woman, it would be worth looking at a similar encounter, this time with a Syro-Phoenician woman in the vicinity of Tyre. That Jesus was even visiting that region is telling in and of itself. It reminds us that despite Jesus's undoubted focus on the house of Israel, he did not restrict it to that. At that moment in the Gospel of Mark he is a considerable distance north, beyond even Galilee. The encounter itself is quite shocking, most of all the imagery Jesus uses to discourage the woman's request for a healing. "Tossing bread to the dogs," which is how Jesus frames the asking, seems derogatory, if not racist. But this is to surely misunderstand his intent—mischievously so, in my opinion. As is often the case, Jesus is not dismissing his interlocutor so much as wanting to elicit a response, which in the case of the Syro-Phoenician woman is a faith every bit as astonishing as the Roman Centurion's faith in Matthew's Gospel. As my friend Dave Hansen once put it in a sermon that I heard him preach in Price Hill Baptist, Cincinnati: she outsmarts Jesus. Her retort that "even the dogs eat the crumbs from under the children's table" is so quick witted, and so utterly determined, that Jesus can do nothing other than relieve the woman's daughter of her demon. And with the closure of the story, we are left wondering what it means to be Israel. In other words, is being Israel a matter of externals—badges of religious observance—or rather, is it something to do with faith in Jesus? In which case, it can happen to anyone, anytime, anywhere.

The fact that Jesus returns to Galilee from his excursion to Tyre, and then into the region of the Decapolis, ought to receive more attention than it does. To those who insist on drawing boundaries, Jesus crosses them as a matter of principle, raising the question as to how an ideology of ethnicity—which is what Christian Zionism is—could ever resonate with such generous catholicity. It is often Paul who is accused of founding a de-ethnicized church, but it turns out that Jesus laid the seeds of

17. Radcliffe and Popko, *Questioning God*, 132.

it. The reason Jesus was driven by the congregation to the edge of the town following his Nazareth sermon is surely because he dared to define the reach of God's grace beyond the borders of Israel.[18] The inclusion of the widow of Zarephath as well as Naaman the Syrian in the Jubilee of God's kingdom is no incidental sermon illustration, but a radical redrawing of boundaries, made more explicit of course in the resurrection and the coming of the Spirit. As Pentecostal scholar Frank Macchia puts it in a chapter on Jesus's Spirit baptism at the Jordan:

> Jesus's particularity however cannot remain within Israel's boundaries, not if it's true to God's promise to the world—and thus to that particularity at its core. The promise is focused on the coming Messiah and the coming Spirit that he will bear and impart. Because the Messiah bears and imparts the cosmic and eschatological Spirit, no nationalism can contain this Messiah without betraying him. No nationalism can seek to domesticate the will of the Creator in pouring forth the divine favour through the Messiah to all nations, for that would quench the Spirit.[19]

Which brings us onto the matter of Romans 9–11. How does this fit within the scheme I am proposing? Here I am putting forward a catholic internationalism on account of the gospel, but here we have a passage in Paul that seems to revert to dyads; gentile expansion leading to Jewish restoration, including the restoration of the land. For my part, I am not convinced that this is the way to read Romans 9–11. Coming after some of the most sophisticated theological argumentation, it would be strange, it seems to me, to revert to some kind of eschatological timeline. The tenor of these chapters is pastoral not sensational. The purpose of the letter, in its entirety, is to unite a community, not trace the future. What is clear, however, regardless of our views about the scale of Jewish conversion, and even its timing, is the fact that the gentiles owe a

---

18. Luke 4:11–30.
19. Macchia, *Jesus the Spirit Baptizer*, 197.

huge debt to the Jews, and but for the hardening of Jewish hearts would have remained outside the promises.

This is not perhaps such a great comfort for Jews, any more than it is for gentiles who have been grafted in, to use the image of the olive tree. The message of God's sovereign plan does not lend itself to easy concepts. But it is at least an acknowledgment that our roots are deeply embedded in an ancient people, whose return to their messiah, whatever that might look like, can only be good news to the world. In fact, to insist on this connection, and to honor it as an integral part of Christian revelation is not inconsequential. Had the church heeded Paul's teaching in these chapters, so much of the sorry and shameful tale of Christian antisemitism might have been avoided. To be grateful for one's roots is to treat them with respect.

Maybe this is what Christian Zionism should be concerned with, and where it has made a positive contribution: not so much a venture forward into end-times but a looking back to where we have come from. In the context of Romans, it ensures that gentile Christianity doesn't see itself as a replacement of the covenant story of God, but rather its continuation. In the context of our own times, to recognize our Jewish roots might strengthen family bonds, open up conversations, and ensure that whatever misgivings we might have about Israeli policies, our thoughts are motivated by friendship, not enmity. Whether that is possible is difficult to say. The cultural moment we are passing through is not conducive to such dialogue. The speed with which ideas are cancelled out is truly shocking. In terms of my own limited constituency, it is likely that my provocations here will be met with disdain. But love always hopes. And my sincerest prayer is that *Beyond Christian Zionism* will stir discussion. I have set out not to offend unnecessarily, nor to speak in triumphalist tones. I am not a replacement theologian, nor an antisemite. I love the Jewish people, just as I love the state of Israel. Like Herzl himself, I don't see the state as a biblical entity but a political reality, and one that should take its place among the nations of the world.[20] To that

20. See Avineri, *Herzl*.

extent, modern Israel is an expression of the sovereign purpose of God—even if what I understand by sovereignty is not quite what Christian Zionists understand by it. Since it is a nation, however, and since it does claim, even in its secularity, some measure of exceptionalism—increasingly so in recent decades—then it is legitimate, in my opinion, to hold its actions up to the light of the traditions from where that exceptionalism came from. The fact that Israelis themselves are doing this is powerful. The battle for the soul of the nation has become an internal argument, which is good. My wish is that Christian Zionists would do something similar.

Epilogue

Wadi Qelt

IN MY PRAYING IMAGINATION over the forty years since my first visit, Wadi Qelt has featured a great deal. A dry river valley in the Judean desert, the defiles becoming deeper the nearer you get to Jericho, it has become for tour guides the location of many episodes in the biblical narrative—so many, in fact, that one wonders what hasn't happened there. According to Wikipedia, it is where Achan was stoned to death; where Elijah lay down under the juniper tree; and where Psalm 23 was written. Personally, I am not sure of any of these, but if a place can be an instantiation of spiritual meaning, beyond even the geographical accuracy of its association, then Wadi Qelt is it. The aridity of the terrain, the silence of the desert, the way the evening sun does indeed create a valleys of shadows, is replete with significance and may explain why I was a little nervous to walk it again, forty years on. The images from my first visit as a nineteen-year-old, including the sighting of the almost mythic St. George's monastery, were so precious to me that I was afraid I would be disappointed on my return. Instead, the walk through the canyon, beginning just south of the inn of the Good Samaritan (near Ma'ale Adumim) and ending in Jericho in the evening, reinforced the images I had been carrying all that time, strengthening not only the memory of them but also their power. After all, forty years is a biblical time frame. It would not have been too far from Wadi Qelt that Jesus recapitulated and redeemed, over a period of forty days, the wilderness wanderings. Like our Lord, I was delighted to leave the wadi with a fresh sense of calling.

Where that calling plays out, I don't know. Like many people, I don't see that much further than the next lily pad in the pond. What I do know, however, is that wherever it plays out, hospitality and generosity need to be at the center of it. The growing internationalism of the church requires it; just as the gospel of Jesus demands it. It is not our business to speculate on end-time scenarios, however fantastical they appear to be. To keep watch over Israel, monitoring every global incident in relation to one's interpretation of biblical prophecy, is a cul-de-sac kind of faith and, by way of further irony, a disservice to both Israelis and Arabs. It's a disservice to Israel because a democracy such as Israel possesses requires flexibility not intransigence. And it's a disservice to Arabs because it hinders the full realization of a Palestinian state. More specifically—and this is where the irony is most disturbing—Christian Zionism encourages the silent but very real disappearance from the Holy Land of the Arab Christian community. Caught between radical Islam on the one hand, and ideological Zionism on the other, it has no place to go other than to vacate. This cannot be an acceptable solution. Christian witness in the Holy Land, both through biblical sites and actual congregational presence, is a constituent part of modern-day Israel, or rather it should be. It surely is part of the genius of the Holy Land. And by genius, I don't mean just tourism, or even pilgrimage, although it is both of those things; but living presence. Without this, something vital is lost to us. Paradoxically, without the particularity of Jesus the Jew—memorialized in the Holy Land through places and people—the universality of Christianity, by which I mean its ability to cross boundaries and appeal to all people, dilutes into something vague. It ceases to be vibrant.

I don't pretend that this heals the rift between Christianity and Judaism. I believe in the uniqueness of Christ and that salvation is through no other name. My Jewish friends respect that, just as I respect that contemporary Judaism is a cultural and community way of life, sometimes quite separate from matters of personal faith. What that means in terms of Christian evangelization, or the honoring of Jewish identity, is for others to write about. What I hope *Beyond Christian Zionism* offers is a way for Christians and Jews, and possibly even Muslims, to identify the true vocation of Israel, which is to love justice, show mercy and walk humbly with our God. Anything that does not align with that, no matter how much it claims biblical legitimacy, is a false religion and a hindrance, not a help, towards the eschatological hope of a redeemed humanity.

As I understand it, this is where the Jewish philosopher Martin Buber arrived at in his own thinking about the land. Regarding Zionism, he was completely committed. In 1944, with the war raging in Europe; news of the extermination of Jews beginning to reach the West; the British administration refusing entry to Jewish refugees, Buber delivered a series of lectures in Jerusalem in which he argued for a number of things:[1] primarily, that the Jews needed to overcome their diaspora mentality and build a country in the land of Israel. In terms of his political orientation, as well as his spiritual vision, this called for a binational state and equal rights for both Jews and Arabs. Crude nationalism, as far as Buber was concerned, was a betrayal of Jewish values. Zionism was not primarily a political issue, nor just a matter of inner spirituality (famously, he said that "Zion must be born in the soul, before it can be created in visible reality") but a community of everyday reality that brings blessing to the world. Interestingly, Buber makes a distinction between "small" and "great" Zionism. Small Zionism, as Buber's biographer Paul Mendes Flohr points out, "deems it sufficient merely to transplant the Jewish people to their ancestral home" in the hope of chartering a happier destiny. The advocates of a great Zionism, however, "want something more: a Jewish commonwealth that will promote the construction of a "'genuine

---

1. Buber, *On Zion*.

human community" (*Gemeinshchaft*),' in accordance with the people of Israel's founding biblical mandate."[2]

Buber, as we know, was not averse to referencing Jesus the Jew in his work. Like many Jewish writers, and even artists, he was able to claim Jesus, so he argued, in a way that is inaccessible for many actual believers. Just so. This may be more common than we gentiles realize. But whether it is, or whether Buber is simply reacting to what he saw as a disturbing trend towards Marcionism in German theology, what I find encouraging when I read Buber is that he imagines for his brand of Zionism what I imagine for the Christian community, especially in its ongoing relationship to Israel. To not have a relationship with Israel, or to think it theologically incidental, is not an option. Even those of us who don't subscribe to a Christian Zionist perspective on the question of land and the return of Christ must embrace the astonishing and often tragic history that led to the creation of the state of Israel in 1948. But what we might also urge, mindful that there is so much at stake theologically in the conflict that began to grow as more and more Jews entered the promised land, is a Zionism that is generous to the world.

Unlike his fellow Zionists, including Herzl of course, Buber saw the struggle for a homeland not as a national struggle, although it could be never less than that, but as a supranational one: "We do not want Palestine for the Jews," he said, "we want it for humankind, for we want it for the realization of Judaism."[3] It is clear from this statement that, for Buber, Zionism is not Judaism—so much so that Buber was urging Ben-Gurion, as late as 1947, to relent from his pursuit of an independent Jewish state, to gather instead around his notion of a binational country, and furthermore, to desist from using the crimes of the Holocaust as the basis for political activism in Palestine.[4] Not surprisingly, Buber lived with the opprobrium of being unpatriotic for the rest of his life. His

2. Mendes-Flohr, *Martin Buber*, 189–90.

3. Quoted in Mendes-Flohr, *Martin Buber*, 115–16.

4. For a longer discussion of these issues, see Mendes-Flohr, *Martin Buber*, 243–58.

antipathy towards Jewish nationalism, and what he regarded as a lack of action on the refugee problem, made him unpopular in those early years of independence. Consequently, he found himself at the margins. But what he highlights is the danger when spiritual vision gets entwined with national ideology. The warning is there at the very beginning of Israel's nation building. As much as the prophet Samuel is a pragmatist and accedes to the request of the people to have a king,[5] nevertheless, he laments the decision, for it represents a departure from the real soul of Israel—a call to rely not upon its own ingenuity but to rely solely and simply on God.

5. 1 Sam 8:21–22.

Appendix 1

Orde Wingate

KNOWN AS THE FATHER of the Israeli Defense Force, British Army Officer Orde Wingate is perhaps one of the most controversial figures in the history of Christian Zionism. Born into a Plymouth Brethren background on February 26, 1903, Wingate was educated at Charterhouse School and the Royal Military Academy in Woolwich. He was later commissioned in the Royal Artillery in 1923. He initially learned Arabic in Sudan, and later fought with the Chindits in Burma, modern-day Myanmar. He also fought against the Arabs in the Middle East.

Wingate didn't seem to be particularly inspired by secular Zionists but was very much a Christian Zionist. An intensely driven man, Wingate truly believed in the divine nature of his mission. He was inspired by a deep love for the Old Testament, so much so that not only did he memorize it but was known to prefer it to the New Testament. Significantly, he regarded himself as a modern-day Gideon. This explains why he would often return to Kibbutz Ein Harod, since it was the area where Gideon fought many of his battles. Some historians, both Israelis as well as Arabs, have accused Wingate of war crimes and atrocities against the Arab population—collective punishment, being the main concern. The so-called night squads, which Wingate pioneered, had a devastating impact on Arab communities. As uncomfortable it is to read, Wingate was known to despise the Arabs, calling them "dirty Arabs."

There is no evidence that Wingate suffered from mental health issues or any kind of psychosis. The issue was more his eccentricity. It is well documented that he used to give speeches to his men standing naked in the shower. For all his eccentricity, however, and his rebellious streak, Wingate was very popular among his men, and was admired by Churchill. He is remembered for his unconventional warfare, and for pioneering surprise attacks. The Israeli Special Forces have a manual which was created by Wingate. There is also the Orde Wingate Institute for Physical Education and Sport, south of Netanya. The Israelis thought very highly of Wingate, and he is revered to this day, particularly in the military. Chaim Weizmann referred to Wingate as the Lawrence of Judea.

Appendix 2

The Complexity of Solidarity

The Baptist Times, October 20, 2023

FORTY YEARS AGO, ON my nineteenth birthday as it happens, I
touched down at Ben Gurion Airport to begin a six-month scholarship with The Friends of Israel: working in a high school in Ashkelon for a couple of months, before moving north to a kibbutz
near Tiberius. Having just come to Christian faith a year earlier,
you can imagine how impressionable I was. I have carried some of
those images with me ever since, not just the obvious ones like the
Sea of Galilee, but the less familiar places like Wadi Qelt, which I
trekked again back in January this year as a kind of pilgrimage to
the faithfulness of God in keeping me all this time. Indeed, the walk
inspired a whole series of reflections, which I wrote up during my
sabbatical this summer, entitled *Beyond Christian Zionism.*

I may as well say now, ahead of publication, that the book
tracks my journey from the heady days of the early eighties when
being an evangelical and pro-Zionist was practically synonymous,
to a situation at present where the welding together of Christian
faith with the expansionist agenda of the Israeli right-wing has
become, for people like me, highly problematic, both hermeneuti-
cally and politically. It's not that visiting the West Bank ten years

ago changed my views. I was already on a journey. But it certainly reinforced my growing conviction that Christian Zionism, at least as far as the Arab Christian community is concerned, is an unhelpful, if not oppressive, theology. The subtitle of the book—*A Travelogue of a Former Ideologue*—says it all, I guess, and serves to get me into trouble, no doubt, since Christian Zionism tends to be very binary, and not given to critique.

Whether it would be wise to publish the book right now, in the light of the horrendous attacks on Israel on 7th October, is a question I am wrestling with. To be honest, the response of the Israeli military to terrorist attacks, which in this instance has already led to the deaths of vast numbers of innocent Palestinians—not to mention the effective demolition of Gaza—is one of the reasons I wrote the book. As a Christian, I find that kind of retaliatory vengeance deeply troubling, even if the enemy is barbaric, and I am not willing to be silent anymore. Collateral damage is too convenient a term to describe the suffering of Palestinian women and children, and one we ought to feel ashamed of. But lest there is any doubt as to my views on the matter, let me also state now that I not only believe in Israel's right to exist, but I also believe it is imperative to say so, and to defend Jews in the incidents of antisemitism that will surely increase in the weeks and months to come. There is no contradiction in such a stance, at least in my opinion. It is an attempt to reflect the complexity of the situation, and the justice issues that resonate not just with the plight of the Palestinians but also the suffering of the Jewish people.

Make no mistake about it, the attacks on Israel by Hamas, the chilling slaughter of Jewish communities in the vicinity of Ashkelon (not forgetting the hostages, of course), are not related to the quest for a two-state solution but nothing short of genocidal, and ought to receive the strongest possible condemnation. That we pray for restraint on the part of the Israeli military is because disproportionality only inflames the very thing it is trying to eradicate. As Bishop George Bell reminded the House of Lords in 1944, with regard to the blanket bombing of German cities, the means by which we prosecute war is as important as its objective. If Israel is to emerge from this war with moral integrity, it must resist at all costs the urge towards barbarism. But to not sympathize, in the first instance, with the existential threat that many Israelis once again fear (and maybe always fear), and which Jews in the diaspora will also share, is not only heartless but, in and of itself, a form of antisemitism. One is not required to be a Christian Zionist to take this line of solidarity. Some of my Jewish friends find Christian Zionism as problematic as I do. They feel like we are instrumentalizing the Jews for our own ends. But to adopt at this time an air of indifference towards Israel, to misunderstand the murderous intent of Hamas, worse still to minimize the significance of what is the largest loss of Jewish life since the Second World War, is to be guilty of a terrible hypocrisy. To speak out against a right-wing government is one thing; and to try to distinguish between Hamas jihadism and long-standing Palestinian political objectives is going to prove important in the days to come. But to not stand now in solidarity with Jewish people, whatever our political and theological opinion, is a dereliction of Christian obligation. I agree with Bonhoeffer, who, writing in the 1930s, said this: "He is no Christian who sings the chants but does not harbour the Jew."

Bibliography

Abuelaish, Izzeldin. *I Shall Not Hate*. London: Bloomsbury, 2011.

Alexander, Sidney. *Marc Chagall: A Biography*. London: Cassels, 1979.

Alter, Robert. *The Book of Psalms: A Translation with Commentary*. New York: Norton, 2007.

Avineri, Shlomo. *Herzl: Theodor Herzl and the Foundation of the Jewish State*. London: Weldenfeld & Nicolson, 2013.

Baddiel, David. *Jews Don't Count: How Identity Politics Failed One Particular Identity*. London: TLS Books, 2022.

Berger, John. *Hold Everything Dear: Dispatches on Survival and Resistance*. London: Verso, 2007.

Borg, Marcus J. *Jesus, a New Vision: Spirit, Culture and The Life of Discipleship*. London: HarperCollins, 1987.

Boyd, Gregory A. *The Myth of a Christian Nation: How the Quest for Political Power Is Destroying the Church*. Grand Rapids: Zondervan, 2005.

Braverman, Mark. *Fatal Embrace: Christians, Jews, and the Search for Peace in the Holy Land*. New York: Beaufort, 2010.

———. *A Wall in Jerusalem: Hope, Healing and the Struggle for Justice in Israel and Palestine*. New York: Jericho, 2013.

Bregman, Ahron. *Cursed Victory: A History of Israel and the Occupied Territories*. London: Allen Lane, 2014.

Bruce, F. F. "Paul and Jerusalem." *Tyndale Bulletin* 19 (1968) 3–25.

Brueggemann, Walter. *Divine Presence Amid Violence: Contextualising the Book of Joshua*. Milton Keynes: Paternoster, 2009.

Buber, Martin. *On Zion: The History of an Idea*. London: Horovitz, 1973.

Burge, Gary M. *Whose Land? Whose Promise? What Christians Are Not Being Told about Israel and the Palestinians*. Milton Keynes: Paternoster, 2003.

Burnett, Ken. *A Nation Called by God: Britain's Leading Role in the Restoration of Israel*. Eastbourne, UK: Love Never Fails, 1983.

Carré, John le. *The Little Drummer Girl*. London: Penguin, 1983.

Carter, Jimmy. *Palestine Peace not Apartheid*. New York: Simon & Schuster, 2007.

Chandler, Andrew. *George Bell, Bishop of Chichester: Church, State, and Resistance in the Age of Dictatorship*. Grand Rapids: Eerdmans, 2016.

Chapman, Colin. *Whose Promised Land?* Tring, UK: Lion, 1983.

Davies, William D. *The Gospel and the Land: Early Christianity and Jewish Territorial Doctrine*. Pantyfedwen Trust Lectures, 1968. Berkeley: University of California Press, 1974.

Dixon, Murray. *Israel: Land of God's Promise*. Lancaster, UK: Sovereign World, 2006.

Fee, Gordon D. *God's Empowering Presence: The Holy Spirit in the Letters of Paul*. Peabody, MA: Hendrickson, 1994.

Figes, Orlando. *Crimea: The Last Crusade*. London: Penguin, 2010.

Friedman, Thomas. *From Beirut to Jerusalem*. New York: Farrar, Strauss & Giroux, 1989.

Giovanni, Janine de. *The Vanishing: The Twilight of Christianity in the Middle East*. London: Bloomsbury, 2021.

Grose, Peter. *The Greatest Escape: How One French Community Saved Thousands of Lives from the Nazis*. London: Nicholas Brealey, 2014.

Hamilton, Jill. *God, Guns and Israel: Britain, the Jews and the First World War*. 3rd ed. Stroud: The History Press, 2009.

Hillesum, Etty. *An Interrupted Life, The Diaries and Letters of Etty Hillesum 1941–43*. Translated by Arnold J. Pomerans. London: Persephone, 1996.

Hocken, Peter. *The Glory and the Shame: Reflections on the 20th-Century Outpouring of the Holy Spirit*. Guildford: Eagle, 1994.

Hurndall, Jocelyn. *Defy the Stars: The Life and Tragic Death of Tom Hurndall*. London: Bloomsbury, 2007.

Hussey, Walter. *Patron of Art: The Revival of a Great Tradition among Modern Artists*. London: Weidenfeld and Nicolson, 1985.

Inchausti, Robert. *Subversive Orthodoxy: Outlaws, Revolutionaries, and Other Christians in Disguise*. Grand Rapids: Brazos, 2005.

Karsh, Efraim. *Palestine Betrayed*. New Haven, CT: Yale University Press, 2011.

Katanacho, Yohanna. *The Land of Christ: A Palestinian Cry*. Eugene, OR: Wipf & Stock, 2013.

Kennedy, Paul. *The Rise and Fall of the Great Powers*. London: Fontana, 1989.

Khalidi, Rashid. *The Hundred Years' War on Palestine: A History of Settler Colonial Conquest and Resistance*. London: Profile, 2020.

King, Martin Luther, Jr. *Strength to Love*. Glasgow: Collins, 1980.

Lambert, Lance. *Battle for Israel*. Eastbourne, UK: Kingsway, 1976.

Levi, Primo. *If This Is a Man and Truce*. London: Abacus, 1979.

Macchia, Frank D. *Jesus the Spirit Baptizer: Christology in the Light of Pentecost*. Grand Rapids: Eerdmans, 2018.

Mayes, Andrew. *Holy Land? Challenging Questions from the Biblical Landscape.* London: SPCK, 2011.

McDermott, Gerald R. *Israel Matters: Why Christians Must Think Differently about the People and the Land.* Grand Rapids: Brazos, 2017.

Mendes-Flohr, Paul. *Martin Buber: A Life of Faith and Dissent.* New Haven, CT: Yale University Press, 2019.

Montefiore, Simon Sebag. *Jerusalem: The Biography.* London: Phoenix, 2011.

Moorhead, Caroline. *The Village of Secrets: Defying the Nazis in Vichy France.* London: Random House, 2014.

Mouw, Richard J. *The Smell of Sawdust: What Evangelicals Can Learn from Their Fundamentalist Heritage:* Grand Rapids: Zondervan, 2000.

Nikondeha, Kelley. *The First Advent in Palestine: Reversals, Resistance, and the Ongoing Complexity of Hope.* Minneapolis: Broadleaf, 2022.

Northcott, Michael. *An Angel Directs the Storm: Apocalyptic Religion and American Empire,* London: Tauris, 2004.

Oz, Amos. *Dear Zealots: Letters from a Divided Land.* London: Chatto & Windus, 2017.

———. *How to Cure a Fanatic: Israel and Palestine: Between Right and Wrong.* London: Vintage, 2012.

———. *A Tale of Love and Darkness.* London: Chatto & Windus, 2003.

Pappe, Ilan *The Ethnic Cleansing of Palestine.* Oxford: Oneworld, 2006.

Patrick, James, ed. *Jesus: King of the Jews? Messianic Judaism, Jewish Christians, and Theology Beyond Supersessionism.* Vienna: Toward Jerusalem Council II, 2021.

Pawson, David. *Defending Christian Zionism.* Anchor Recordings, 2014.

Peterson, Eugene H. *Under the Unpredictable Plant: An Exploration in Vocational Holiness.* Grand Rapids: Eerdmans, 1992.

Pfeffer, Anshel. *Bibi: The Turbulent Life and Times of Benjamin Netanyahu.* London: Hurst, 2018.

Potok, Chaim. *The Chosen.* London: Penguin, 1970.

Prince, Derek. *The Last Word on the Middle East.* Eastbourne, UK: Kingsway, 1982.

———. *Why Israel? God's Heart for a People, His Plan for a Nation.* N.p.: Derek Prince Ministries, 2018.

Price, Stanley, and Munro Price. *The Road to the Apocalypse: The Extraordinary Journey of Lewis Way.* London: Notting Hill, 2011.

Radcliffe, Timothy, and Łukasz Popko. *Questioning God.* London: Bloomsbury Continuum, 2023.

Raphael, Melissa. *The Female Face of God in Auschwitz: A Jewish Feminist Theology of the Holocaust.* Abingdon, UK: Routledge, 2003.

Rodinson, Maxime. *Israel and the Arabs.* London: Penguin, 1973.

Russell, Gerard. *Heirs to Forgotten Kingdoms: Journeys into the Disappearing Religions of the Middle East.* London: Simon & Schuster, 2014.

Ryan, Jordan J. *From the Passion to the Church of the Holy Sepulchre: Memories of Jesus in Place, Pilgrimage, and Early Holy Sites over the First Three Centuries.* London: T. & T. Clark, 2022.

Sacks, Jonathan. *Future Tense: A Vision for Jews and Judaism in the Global Culture.* London: Hodder & Stoughton, 2009.

———. *Not in God's Name: Confronting Religious Violence.* London: Hodder and Stoughton, 2015.

Sand, Shlomo. *The Invention of the Land of Israel: From Holy Land to Homeland.* London: Verso, 2012.

Schama, Simon. *Landscape and Memory.* London: Fontana, 1995.

Schama, Simon, and Anthony Julias. "John Berger Is Wrong." *The Guardian,* December 22, 2006.

Segev, Tom. *A State at any Cost: The Life of David Ben-Gurion.* London: Apollo, 2019.

Shavit, Ari. *My Promised Land: The Triumph and Tragedy of Israel.* London: Scribe, 2013.

Sizer, Stephen. *Christian Zionism: Road-map to Armageddon.* Downers Grove, IL: InterVarsity, 2004.

Torrance, David, and George Taylor. *Israel, God's Servant: God's Key to the Redemption of the World.* Milton Keynes: Paternoster, 2007.

Walker, P. W. L. *Jesus and the Holy City: New Testament Perspectives on Jerusalem.* Grand Rapids: Eerdmans, 1996.

Ward, W. R. *The Protestant Evangelical Awakening.* Cambridge: Cambridge University Press, 1998.

Westcott, B. F. *The Gospel according to John.* London: John Murray, 1889.

Wiesel, Elie. *Night.* London: Penguin, 2008.

Wright, N. T. *The Climax of the Covenant: Christ and the Law in Pauline Theology.* Minneapolis: Fortress, 1992.

———. *Paul.* London: SPCK, 2020.

White, Ben. *Israeli Apartheid: A Beginner's Guide.* London: Pluto, 2009.

Wullschlager, Jackie. *Chagall: Love and Exile.* London: Allen Lane, 2008.

Zuabi, Amir Nizar. *I Am Yusuf and This Is My Brother.* London: Methuen Drama, 2009.